DAN-1   DANTES SUBJECT STANDARDIZED TESTS (DSST)

This is your
PASSBOOK for...

Astronomy

Test Preparation Study Guide
Questions & Answers

COPYRIGHT NOTICE

This book is SOLELY intended for, is sold ONLY to, and its use is RESTRICTED to individual, bona fide applicants or candidates who qualify by virtue of having seriously filed applications for appropriate license, certificate, professional and/or promotional advancement, higher school matriculation, scholarship, or other legitimate requirements of education and/or governmental authorities.

This book is NOT intended for use, class instruction, tutoring, training, duplication, copying, reprinting, excerption, or adaptation, etc., by:

1) Other publishers
2) Proprietors and/or Instructors of "Coaching" and/or Preparatory Courses
3) Personnel and/or Training Divisions of commercial, industrial, and governmental organizations
4) Schools, colleges, or universities and/or their departments and staffs, including teachers and other personnel
5) Testing Agencies or Bureaus
6) Study groups which seek by the purchase of a single volume to copy and/or duplicate and/or adapt this material for use by the group as a whole without having purchased individual volumes for each of the members of the group
7) Et al.

Such persons would be in violation of appropriate Federal and State statutes.

PROVISION OF LICENSING AGREEMENTS – Recognized educational, commercial, industrial, and governmental institutions and organizations, and others legitimately engaged in educational pursuits, including training, testing, and measurement activities, may address request for a licensing agreement to the copyright owners, who will determine whether, and under what conditions, including fees and charges, the materials in this book may be used them. In other words, a licensing facility exists for the legitimate use of the material in this book on other than an individual basis. However, it is asseverated and affirmed here that the material in this book CANNOT be used without the receipt of the express permission of such a licensing agreement from the Publishers. Inquiries re licensing should be addressed to the company, attention rights and permissions department.

All rights reserved, including the right of reproduction in whole or in part, in any form or by any means, electronic or mechanical, including photocopying, recording, or by any information storage and retrieval system, without permission in writing from the Publisher.

Copyright © 2025 by
National Learning Corporation

212 Michael Drive, Syosset, NY 11791
(516) 921-8888 • www.passbooks.com
E-mail: info@passbooks.com

PASSBOOK® SERIES

THE *PASSBOOK® SERIES* has been created to prepare applicants and candidates for the ultimate academic battlefield – the examination room.

At some time in our lives, each and every one of us may be required to take an examination – for validation, matriculation, admission, qualification, registration, certification, or licensure.

Based on the assumption that every applicant or candidate has met the basic formal educational standards, has taken the required number of courses, and read the necessary texts, the *PASSBOOK® SERIES* furnishes the one special preparation which may assure passing with confidence, instead of failing with insecurity. Examination questions – together with answers – are furnished as the basic vehicle for study so that the mysteries of the examination and its compounding difficulties may be eliminated or diminished by a sure method.

This book is meant to help you pass your examination provided that you qualify and are serious in your objective.

The entire field is reviewed through the huge store of content information which is succinctly presented through a provocative and challenging approach – the question-and-answer method.

A climate of success is established by furnishing the correct answers at the end of each test.

You soon learn to recognize types of questions, forms of questions, and patterns of questioning. You may even begin to anticipate expected outcomes.

You perceive that many questions are repeated or adapted so that you can gain acute insights, which may enable you to score many sure points.

You learn how to confront new questions, or types of questions, and to attack them confidently and work out the correct answers.

You note objectives and emphases, and recognize pitfalls and dangers, so that you may make positive educational adjustments.

Moreover, you are kept fully informed in relation to new concepts, methods, practices, and directions in the field.

You discover that you are actually taking the examination all the time: you are preparing for the examination by "taking" an examination, not by reading extraneous and/or supererogatory textbooks.

In short, this PASSBOOK®, used directedly, should be an important factor in helping you to pass your test.

NONTRADITIONAL EDUCATION

Students returning to school as adults bring more varied experience to their studies than do the teenagers who begin college shortly after graduating from high school. As a result, there are numerous programs for students with nontraditional learning curves. Hundreds of colleges and universities grant degrees to people who cannot attend classes at a regular campus or have already learned what the college is supposed to teach.

You can earn nontraditional education credits in many ways:
- Passing standardized exams
- Demonstrating knowledge gained through experience
- Completing campus-based coursework, and
- Taking courses off campus

Some methods of assessing learning for credit are objective, such as standardized tests. Others are more subjective, such as a review of life experiences.

With some help from four hypothetical characters – Alice, Vin, Lynette, and Jorge – this article describes nontraditional ways of earning educational credit. It begins by describing programs in which you can earn a high school diploma without spending 4 years in a classroom. The college picture is more complicated, so it is presented in two parts: one on gaining credit for what you know through course work or experience, and a second on college degree programs. The final section lists resources for locating more information.

Earning High School Credit

People who were prevented from finishing high school as teenagers have several options if they want to do so as adults. Some major cities have back-to-school programs that allow adults to attend high school classes with current students. But the more practical alternatives for most adults are to take the General Educational Development (GED) tests or to earn a high school diploma by demonstrating their skills or taking correspondence classes.

Of course, these options do not match the experience of staying in high school and graduating with one's friends. But they are viable alternatives for adult learners committed to meeting and, often, continuing their educational goals.

GED Program

Alice quit high school her sophomore year and took a job to help support herself, her younger brother, and their newly widowed mother. Now an adult, she wants to earn her high school diploma – and then go on to college. Because her job as head cook and her family responsibilities keep her busy during the day, she plans to get a high school equivalency diploma. She will study for, and take, the GED tests. Every year, about half a million adults earn their high school credentials this way. A GED diploma is accepted in lieu of a high school one by more than 90 percent of employers, colleges, and universities, so it is a good choice for someone like Alice.

The GED testing program is sponsored by the American Council on Education and State and local education departments. It consists of examinations in five subject areas: Writing, science, mathematics, social studies, and literature and the arts. The tests also measure skills such as analytical ability, problem solving, reading comprehension, and ability to understand and apply information. Most of the questions are multiple choice; the writing test includes an essay section on a topic of general interest.

Eligibility rules for taking the exams vary, but some states require that you must be at least 18. Tests are given in English, Spanish, and French. In addition to standard print, versions in large print, Braille, and audiocassette are also available. Total time allotted for the tests is 7 1/2 hours.

The GED tests are not easy. About one-fourth of those who complete the exams every year do not pass. Passing scores are established by administering the tests to a sample of graduating high school seniors. The minimum standard score is set so that about one-third of graduating seniors would not pass the tests if they took them.

Because of the difficulty of the tests, people need to prepare themselves to take them. Often, they start by taking the Official GED Practice Tests, usually available through a local adult education center. Centers are listed in your phone book's blue pages under "Adult Education," "Continuing Education," or "GED." Adult education centers also have information about GED preparation classes and self-study materials. Classes are generally arranged to accommodate adults' work schedules. National Learning Corporation publishes several study guides that aim to thoroughly prepare test-takers for the GED.

School districts, colleges, adult education centers, and community organizations have information about GED testing schedules and practice tests. For more information, contact them, your nearest GED testing center, or:

GED Testing Service
One Dupont Circle, NW, Suite 250
Washington, DC 20036-1163
1(800) 62-MY GED (626-9433)
(202) 939-9490

Skills Demonstration

Adults who have acquired high school level skills through experience might be eligible for the National External Diploma Program. This alternative to the GED does not involve any direct instruction. Instead, adults seeking a high school diploma must demonstrate mastery of 65 competencies in 8 general areas: Communication; computation; occupational preparedness; and self, social, consumer, scientific, and technological awareness.

Mastery is shown through the completion of the tasks. For example, a participant could prove competency in computation by measuring a room for carpeting, figuring out the amount of carpet needed, and computing the cost.

Before being accepted for the program, adults undergo an evaluation. Tests taken at one of the program's offices measure reading, writing, and mathematics abilities. A take-home segment includes a self-assessment of current skills, an individual skill evaluation, and an occupational interest and aptitude test.

Adults accepted for the program have weekly meetings with an assessor. At the meeting, the assessor reviews the participant's work from the previous week. If the task has not been completed properly, the assessor explains the mistake. Participants continue to correct their errors until they master each competency. A high school diploma is awarded upon proven mastery of all 65 competencies.

Fourteen States and the District of Columbia now offer the External Diploma Program. For more information, contact:
External Diploma Program
One Dupont Circle, NW, Suite 250
Washington, DC 20036-1193
(202) 939-9475

Correspondence and Distance Study
Vin dropped out of high school during his junior year because his family's frequent moves made it difficult for him to continue his studies. He promised himself at the time he dropped out that he would someday finish the courses needed for his diploma. For people like Vin, who prefer to earn a traditional diploma in a nontraditional way, there are about a dozen accredited courses of study for earning a high school diploma by correspondence, or distance study. The programs are either privately run, affiliated with a university, or administered by a State education department.

Distance study diploma programs have no residency requirements, allowing students to continue their studies from almost any location. Depending on the course of study, students need not be enrolled full time and usually have more flexible schedules for finishing their work. Selection of courses ranges from vo-tech to college prep, and some programs place different emphasis on the types of diplomas offered. University affiliated schools, for example, allow qualified students to take college courses along with their high school ones. Students can then apply the college credits toward a degree at that university or transfer them to another institution.

Taking courses by distance study is often more challenging and time consuming than attending classes, especially for adults who have other obligations. Success depends on each student's motivation. Students usually do reading assignments on their own. Written exercises, which they complete and send to an instructor for grading, supplement their reading material.

A list of some accredited high schools that offer diplomas by distance study is available free from the Distance Education and Training Council, formerly known as the National Home Study Council. Request the "DETC Directory of Accredited Institutions" from:
The Distance Education and Training Council
1601 18th Street, NW.
Washington, DC 20009-2529
(202) 234-5100

Some publications profiling nontraditional college programs include addresses and descriptions of several high school correspondence ones. See the Resources section at the end of this article for more information.

Getting College Credit For What You Know
Adults can receive college credit for prior coursework, by passing examinations, and documenting experiential learning. With help from a college advisor, nontraditional students should assess their skills, establish their educational goals, and determine the number of college credits they might be eligible for.

Even before you meet with a college advisor, you should collect all your school and training records. Then, make a list of all knowledge and abilities acquired through experience, no matter how irrelevant they seem to your chosen field. Next, determine your educational goals: What specific field do you wish to study? What kind of a degree do you want? Finally, determine how your past work fits into the field of study. Later on, you will evaluate educational programs to find one that's right for you.

People who have complex educational or experiential learning histories might want to have their learning evaluated by the Regents Credit Bank. The Credit Bank, operated by Regents College of the University of the State of New York, allows people to consolidate credits earned through college, experience, or other methods. Special assessments are available for Regents College enrollees whose knowledge in a specific field cannot be adequately evaluated by standardized exams. For more information, contact the Regents Credit Bank at:

Regents College
7 Columbia Circle
Albany, NY 12203-5159
(518) 464-8500

Credit For Prior College Coursework

When Lynette was in college during the 1970s, she attended several different schools and took a variety of courses. She did well in some classes and poorly in others. Now that she is a successful business owner and has more focus, Lynette thinks she should forget about her previous coursework and start from scratch. Instead, she should start from where she is.

Lynette should have all her transcripts sent to the colleges or universities of her choice and let an admissions officer determine which classes are applicable toward a degree. A few credits here and there may not seem like much, but they add up. Even if the subjects do not seem relevant to any major, they might be counted as elective credits toward a degree. And comparing the cost of transcripts with the cost of college courses, it makes sense to spend a few dollars per transcript for a chance to save hundreds, and perhaps thousands, of dollars in books and tuition.

Rules for transferring credits apply to all prior coursework at accredited colleges and universities, whether done on campus or off. Courses completed off campus, often called extended learning, include those available to students through independent study and correspondence. Many schools have extended learning programs; Brigham Young University, for example, offers more than 300 courses through its Department of Independent Study. One type of extended learning is distance learning, a form of correspondence study by technological means such as television, video and audio, CD-ROM, electronic mail, and computer tutorials. See the Resources section at the end of this article for more information about publications available from the National University Continuing Education Association.

Any previously earned college credits should be considered for transfer, no matter what the subject or the grade received. Many schools do not accept the transfer of courses graded below a C or ones taken more than a designated number of years ago. Some colleges and universities also have limits on the number of credits that can be transferred and applied toward a degree. But not all do. For example, Thomas Edison State College, New Jersey's State college for adults, accepts the transfer of all 120 hours of credit required for a baccalaureate degree – provided all the credits are transferred from regionally accredited schools, no more than 80 are at the junior college level, and the student's grades overall and in the field of study average out to C.

To assign credit for prior coursework, most schools require original transcripts. This means you must complete a form or send a written, signed request to have your transcripts released directly to a college or university. Once you have chosen the schools you want to apply to, contact the schools you attended before. Find out how much each transcript costs, and ask them to send your transcripts to the ones you are applying to. Write a letter that includes your name (and names used during attendance, if different) and dates of attendance, along with the names and addresses of the schools to which your transcripts should be sent. Include payment and mail to the registrar at the schools you have attended. The registrar's office will process your request and send an official transcript of your coursework to the colleges or universities you have designated.

Credit For Noncollege Courses

Colleges and universities are not the only ones that offer classes. Volunteer organizations and employers often provide formal training worth college credit. The American Council on Education has two programs that assess thousands of specific courses and make recommendations on the amount of college credit they are worth. Colleges and universities accept the recommendations or use them as guidelines.

One program evaluates educational courses sponsored by government agencies, business and industry, labor unions, and professional and voluntary organizations. It is the Program on Noncollegiate Sponsored Instruction (PONSI). Some of the training seminars Alice has participated in covered topics such as food preparation, kitchen safety, and nutrition. Although she has not yet earned her GED, Alice can earn college credit because of her completion of these formal job-training seminars. The number of credits each seminar is worth does not hinge on Alice's current eligibility for college enrollment.

The other program evaluates courses offered by the Army, Navy, Air Force, Marines, Coast Guard, and Department of Defense. It is the Military Evaluations Program. Jorge has never attended college, but the engineering technology classes he completed as part of his military training are worth college credit. And as an Army veteran, Jorge is eligible for a service that takes the evaluations one step further. The Army/American Council on Education Registry Transcript System (AARTS) will provide Jorge with an individualized transcript of American Council on Education credit recommendations for all courses he completed, the military occupational specialties (MOS's) he held, and examinations he passed while in the Army. All Army and National Guard enlisted personnel and veterans who enlisted after October 1981 are eligible for the transcript. Similar services are being considered by the Navy and Marine Corps.

To obtain a free transcript, see your Army Education Center for a 5454R transcript request form. Include your name, Social Security number, basic active service date, and complete address where you want the transcript sent. Mail your request to:
AARTS Operations Center
415 McPherson Ave.
Fort Leavenworth, KS 66027-1373

Recommendations for PONSI are published in *The National Guide to Educational Credit for Training Programs;* military program recommendations are in *The Guide to the Evaluation of Educational Experiences in the Armed Forces.* See the Resources section at the end of this article for more information about these publications.

Former military personnel who took a foreign language course through the Defense Language Institute may request course transcripts by sending their name, Social Security number, course title, duration of the course, and graduation date to:

    Commandant, Defense Language Institute
    Attn: ATFL-DAA-AR
    Transcripts
    Presidio of Monterey
    Monterey, CA 93944-5006

Not all of Jorge's and Alice's courses have been assessed by the American Council on Education. Training courses that have no Council credit recommendation should still be assessed by an advisor at the schools they want to attend. Course descriptions, class notes, test scores, and other documentation may be helpful for comparing training courses to their college equivalents. An oral examination or other demonstration of competency might also be required.

There is no guarantee you will receive all the credits you are seeking – but you certainly won't if you make no attempt.

Credit By Examination

Standardized tests are the best-known method of receiving college credit without taking courses. These exams are often taken by high school students seeking advanced placement for college, but they are also available to adult learners. Testing programs and colleges and universities offer exams in a number of subjects. Two U.S. Government institutes have foreign language exams for employees that also may be worth college credit.

It is important to understand that receiving a passing score on these exams does not mean you get college credit automatically. Each school determines which test results it will accept, minimum scores required, how scores are converted for credit, and the amount of credit, if any, to be assigned. Most colleges and universities accept the American Council on Education credit recommendations, published every other year in the 250-page *Guide to Educational Credit by Examination*. For more information, contact:

    The American Council on Education
    Credit by Examination Program
    One Dupont Circle, Suite 250
    Washington, DC 20036-1193
    (202) 939-9434

Testing programs:

You might know some of the five national testing programs by their acronyms or initials: CLEP, ACT PEP: RCE, DANTES, AP, and NOCTI. (The meanings of these initialisms are explained below.) There is some overlap among programs; for example, four of them have introductory accounting exams. Since you will not be awarded credit more than once for a specific subject, you should carefully evaluate each program for the subject exams you wish to take. And before taking an exam, make sure you will be awarded credit by the college or university you plan to attend.

CLEP (College-Level Examination Program), administered by the College Board, is the most widely accepted of the national testing programs; more than 2,800 accredited schools award credit for passing exam scores. Each test covers material taught in basic undergraduate courses. There are five general exams – English composition, humanities, college mathematics, natural sciences, and social sciences and history – and many subject exams. Most exams are entirely multiple-choice, but English composition exams may include an essay section. For more information, contact:

    CLEP
    P.O. Box 6600
    Princeton, NJ 08541-6600
    (609) 771-7865

ACT PEP: RCE (American College Testing Proficiency Exam Program: Regents College Examinations) tests are given in 38 subjects within arts and sciences, business, education, and nursing. Each exam is recommended for either lower- or upper-level credit. Exams contain either objective or extended response questions, and are graded according to a standard score, letter grade, or pass/fail. Fees vary, depending on the subject and type of exam. For more information or to request free study guides, contact:

    ACT PEP: Regents College Examinations
    P.O. Box 4014
    Iowa City, IA 52243
    (319) 337-1387
    (New York State residents must contact Regents College directly.)

DANTES (Defense Activity for Nontraditional Education Support) standardized tests are developed by the Educational Testing Service for the Department of Defense. Originally administered only to military personnel, the exams have been available to the public since 1983. About 50 subject tests cover business, mathematics, social science, physical science, humanities, foreign languages, and applied technology. Most of the tests consist entirely of multiple-choice questions. Schools determine their own administering fees and testing schedules. For more information or to request free study sheets, contact:

    DANTES Program Office
    Mail Stop 31-X
    Educational Testing Service
    Princeton, NJ 08541
    1(800) 257-9484

The AP (Advanced Placement) Program is a cooperative effort between secondary schools and colleges and universities. AP exams are developed each year by committees of college and high school faculty appointed by the College Board and assisted by consultants from the Educational Testing Service. Subjects include arts and languages, natural sciences, computer science, social sciences, history, and mathematics. Most tests are 2 or 3 hours long and include both multiple-choice and essay questions. AP courses are available to help students prepare for exams, which are offered in the spring. For more information about the Advanced Placement Program, contact:

    Advanced Placement Services
    P.O. Box 6671
    Princeton, NJ 08541-6671
    (609) 771-7300

NOCTI (National Occupational Competency Testing Institute) assessments are designed for people like Alice, who have vocational-technical skills that cannot be evaluated by other tests. NOCTI assesses competency at two levels: Student/job ready and teacher/experienced worker. Standardized evaluations are available for occupations such as auto-body repair, electronics, mechanical drafting, quantity food preparation, and upholstering. The tests consist of multiple-choice questions and a performance component. Other services include workshops, customized assessments, and pre-testing. For more information, contact:

NOCTI
500 N. Bronson Ave.
Ferris State University
Big Rapids, MI 49307
(616) 796-4699

Colleges and universities:

Many colleges and universities have credit-by-exam programs, through which students earn credit by passing a comprehensive exam for a course offered by the institution. Among the most widely recognized are the programs at Ohio University, the University of North Carolina, Thomas Edison State College, and New York University.

Ohio University offers about 150 examinations for credit. In addition, you may sometimes arrange to take special examinations in non-laboratory courses offered at Ohio University. To take a test for credit, you must enroll in the course. If you plan to transfer the credit earned, you also need written permission from an official at your school. Books and study materials are available, for a cost, through the university. Exams must be taken within 6 months of the enrollment date; most last 3 hours. You may arrange to take the exam off campus if you do not live near the university.

Ohio University is on the quarter-hour system; most courses are worth 4 quarter hours, the equivalent of 3 semester hours. For more information, contact:

Independent Study
Tupper Hall 302
Ohio University
Athens, OH 45701-2979
1(800) 444-2910
(614) 593-2910

The University of North Carolina offers a credit-by-examination option for 140 independent study (correspondence) courses in foreign languages, humanities, social sciences, mathematics, business administration, education, electrical and computer engineering, health administration, and natural sciences. To take an exam, you must request and receive approval from both the course instructor and the independent studies department. Exams must be taken within six months of enrollment, and you may register for no more than two at a time. If you are not near the University's Chapel Hill campus, you may take your exam under supervision at an accredited college, university, community college, or technical institute. For more information, contact:

Independent Studies
CB #1020, The Friday Center
UNC-Chapel Hill
Chapel Hill, NC 27599-1020
1(800) 862-5669 / (919) 962-1134

The Thomas Edison College Examination Program offers more than 50 exams in liberal arts, business, and professional areas. Thomas Edison State College administers tests twice a month in Trenton, New Jersey; however, students may arrange to take their tests with a proctor at any accredited American college or university or U.S. military base. Most of the tests are multiple choice; some also include short answer or essay questions. Time limits range from 90 minutes to 4 hours, depending on the exam. For more information, contact:

Thomas Edison State College
TECEP, Office of Testing and Assessment
101 W. State Street
Trenton, NJ 08608-1176
(609) 633-2844

New York University's Foreign Language Program offers proficiency exams in more than 40 languages, from Albanian to Yiddish. Two exams are available in each language: The 12-point test is equivalent to 4 undergraduate semesters, and the 16-point exam may lead to upper level credit. The tests are given at the university's Foreign Language Department throughout the year.

Proof of foreign language proficiency does not guarantee college credit. Some colleges and universities accept transcripts only for languages commonly taught, such as French and Spanish. Nontraditional programs are more likely than traditional ones to grant credit for proficiency in other languages.

For an informational brochure and registration form for NYU's foreign language proficiency exams, contact:

New York University
Foreign Language Department
48 Cooper Square, Room 107
New York, NY 10003
(212) 998-7030

Government institutes:
The Defense Language Institute and Foreign Service Institute administer foreign language proficiency exams for personnel stationed abroad. Usually, the tests are given at the end of intensive language courses or upon completion of service overseas. But some people -- like Jorge, who knows Spanish -- speak another language fluently and may be allowed to take a proficiency exam in that language before completing their tour of duty. Contact one of the offices listed below to obtain transcripts of those scores. Proof of proficiency does not guarantee college credit, however, as discussed above.

To request score reports from the Defense Language Institute for Defense Language Proficiency Tests, send your name, Social Security number, language for which you were tested, and, most importantly, when and where you took the exam to:

Commandant, Defense Language Institute
Attn: ATFL-ES-T
DLPT Score Report Request
Presidio of Monterey
Monterey, CA 93944-5006

To request transcripts of scores for Foreign Service Institute exams, send your name, Social Security number, language for which you were tested, and dates or year of exams to:

Foreign Service Institute
Arlington Hall
4020 Arlington Boulevard
Rosslyn, VA 22204-1500
Attn: Testing Office (Send your request to the attention of the testing office of the foreign language in which you were tested)

Credit For Experience

Experiential learning credit may be given for knowledge gained through job responsibilities, personal hobbies, volunteer opportunities, homemaking, and other experiences. Colleges and universities base credit awards on the knowledge you have attained, not for the experience alone. In addition, the knowledge must be college level; not just any learning will do. Throwing horseshoes as a hobby is not likely to be worth college credit. But if you've done research on how and where the sport originated, visited blacksmiths, organized tournaments, and written a column for a trade journal – well, that's a horseshoe of a different color.

Adults attempting to get credit for their experience should be forewarned: Having your experience evaluated for college credit is time-consuming, tedious work – not an easy shortcut for people who want quick-fix college credits. And not all experience, no matter how valuable, is the equivalent of college courses.

Requesting college credit for your experiential learning can be tricky. You should get assistance from a credit evaluations officer at the school you plan to attend, but you should also have a general idea of what your knowledge is worth. A common method for converting knowledge into credit is to use a college catalog. Find course titles and descriptions that match what you have learned through experience, and request the number of credits offered for those courses.

Once you know what credit to ask for, you must usually present your case in writing to officials at the college you plan to attend. The most common form of presenting experiential learning for credit is the portfolio. A portfolio is a written record of your knowledge along with a request for equivalent college credit. It includes an identification and description of the knowledge for which you are requesting credit, an explanatory essay of how the knowledge was gained and how it fits into your educational plans, documentation that you have acquired such knowledge, and a request for college credit. Required elements of a portfolio vary by schools but generally follow those guidelines.

In identifying knowledge you have gained, be specific about exactly what you have learned. For example, it is not enough for Lynette to say she runs a business. She must identify the knowledge she has gained from running it, such as personnel management, tax law, marketing strategy, and inventory review. She must also include brief descriptions about her knowledge of each to support her claims of having those skills.

The essay gives you a chance to relay something about who you are. It should address your educational goals, include relevant autobiographical details, and be well organized, neat, and convey confidence. In his essay, Jorge might first state his goal of becoming an engineer. Then he would explain why he joined the Army, where he got hands-on training and experience in developing and servicing electronic equipment.

This, he would say, led to his hobby of creating remote-controlled model cars, of which he has built 20. His conclusion would highlight his accomplishments and tie them to his desire to become an electronic engineer.

Documentation is evidence that you've learned what you claim to have learned. You can show proof of knowledge in a variety of ways, including audio or video recordings, letters from current or former employers describing your specific duties and job performance, blueprints, photographs or artwork, and transcripts of certifying exams for professional licenses and certification – such as Alice's certification from the American Culinary Federation. Although documentation can take many forms, written proof alone is not always enough. If it is impossible to document your knowledge in writing, find out if your experiential learning can be assessed through supplemental oral exams by a faculty expert.

Earning a College Degree

Nontraditional students often have work, family, and financial obligations that prevent them from quitting their jobs to attend school full time. Can they still meet their educational goals? Yes.

More than 150 accredited colleges and universities have nontraditional bachelor's degree programs that require students to spend little or no time on campus; over 300 others have nontraditional campus-based degree programs. Some of those schools, as well as most junior and community colleges, offer associate's degrees nontraditionally. Each school with a nontraditional course of study determines its own rules for awarding credit for prior coursework, exams, or experience, as discussed previously. Most have charges on top of tuition for providing these special services.

Several publications profile nontraditional degree programs; see the Resources section at the end of this article for more information. To determine which school best fits your academic profile and educational goals, first list your criteria. Then, evaluate nontraditional programs based on their accreditation, features, residency requirements, and expenses. Once you have chosen several schools to explore further, write to them for more information. Detailed explanations of school policies should help you decide which ones you want to apply to.

Get beyond the printed word – especially the glowing words each school writes about itself. Check out the schools you are considering with higher education authorities, alumni, employers, family members, and friends. If possible, visit the campus to talk to students and instructors and sit in on a few classes, even if you will be completing most or all of your work off campus. Ask school officials questions about such things as enrollment numbers, graduation rate, faculty qualifications, and confusing details about the application process or academic policies. After you have thoroughly investigated each prospective college or university, you can make an informed decision about which is right for you.

Accreditation

Accreditation is a process colleges and universities submit to voluntarily for getting their credentials. An accredited school has been investigated and visited by teams of observers and has periodic inspections by a private accrediting agency. The initial review can take two years or more.

Regional agencies accredit entire schools, and professional agencies accredit either specialized schools or departments within schools. Although there are no national accrediting standards, not just any accreditation will do. Countless "accreditation associations" have been invented by schools, many of which have no academic programs and sell phony degrees, to accredit themselves. But 6 regional and about 80 professional accrediting associations in the United States are recognized by the U.S. Department of Education or the Commission on Recognition of Postsecondary Accreditation. When checking accreditation, these are the names to look for. For more information about accreditation and accrediting agencies, contact:

Institutional Participation Oversight Service Accreditation and State Liaison Division
U.S. Department of Education
ROB 3, Room 3915
600 Independence Ave., SW
Washington, DC 20202-5244
(202) 708-7417

Because accreditation is not mandatory, lack of accreditation does not necessarily mean a school or program is bad. Some schools choose not to apply for accreditation, are in the process of applying, or have educational methods too unconventional for an accrediting association's standards. For the nontraditional student, however, earning a degree from a college or university with recognized accreditation is an especially important consideration. Although nontraditional education is becoming more widely accepted, it is not yet mainstream. Employers skeptical of a degree earned in a nontraditional manner are likely to be even less accepting of one from an unaccredited school.

Program Features

Because nontraditional students have diverse educational objectives, nontraditional schools are diverse in what they offer. Some programs are geared toward helping students organize their scattered educational credits to get a degree as quickly as possible. Others cater to those who may have specific credits or experience but need assistance in completing requirements. Whatever your educational profile, you should look for a program that works with you in obtaining your educational goals.

A few nontraditional programs have special admissions policies for adult learners like Alice, who plan to earn their GEDs but want to enroll in college in the meantime. Other features of nontraditional programs include individualized learning agreements, intensive academic counseling, cooperative learning and internship placement, and waiver of some prerequisites or other requirements – as well as college credit for prior coursework, examinations, and experiential learning, all discussed previously.

Lynette, whose primary goal is to finish her degree, wants to earn maximum credits for her business experience. She will look for programs that do not limit the number of credits awarded for equivalency exams and experiential learning. And since well-documented proof of knowledge is essential for earning experiential learning credits, Lynette should make sure the program she chooses provides assistance to students submitting a portfolio.

Jorge, on the other hand, has more credits than he needs in certain areas and is willing to forego some. To become an engineer, he must have a bachelor's degree; but because he is accustomed to hands-on learning, Jorge is interested in getting experience as he gains more technical skills. He will concentrate on finding schools with strong cooperative education, supervised fieldwork, or internship programs.

Residency Requirements

Programs are sometimes deemed nontraditional because of their residency requirements. Many people think of residency for colleges and universities in terms of tuition, with in-state students paying less than out-of-state ones. Residency also may refer to where a student lives, either on or off campus, while attending school.

But in nontraditional education, residency usually refers to how much time students must spend on campus, regardless of whether they attend classes there. In some nontraditional programs, students need not ever step foot on campus. Others require only a very short residency, such as one day or a few weeks. Many schools have standard residency requirements of several semesters but schedule classes for evenings or weekends to accommodate working adults.

Lynette, who previously took courses by independent study, prefers to earn credits by distance study. She will focus on schools that have no residency requirement. Several colleges and universities have nonresident degree completion programs for adults with some college credit. Under the direction of a faculty advisor, students devise a plan for earning their remaining credits. Methods for earning credits include independent study, distance learning, seminars, supervised fieldwork, and group study at arranged sites. Students may have to earn a certain number of credits through the degree-granting institution. But many programs allow students to take courses at accredited schools of their choice for transfer toward their degree.

Alice wants to attend lectures but has an unpredictable schedule. Her best course of action will be to seek out short residency programs that require students to attend seminars once or twice a semester. She can take courses that are televised and videotape them to watch when her schedule permits, with the seminars helping to ensure that she properly completes her coursework. Many colleges and universities with short residency requirements also permit students to earn some credits elsewhere, by whatever means the student chooses.

Some fields of study require classroom instruction. As Jorge will discover, few colleges and universities allow students to earn a bachelor's degree in engineering entirely through independent study. Nontraditional residency programs are designed to accommodate adults' daytime work schedules. Jorge should look for programs offering evening, weekend, summer, and accelerated courses.

Tuition and Other Expenses

The final decisions about which schools Alice, Jorge, and Lynette attend may hinge in large part on a single issue: Cost. And rising tuition is only part of the equation. Beginning with application fees and continuing through graduation fees, college expenses add up.

Traditional and nontraditional students have some expenses in common, such as the cost of books and other materials. Tuition might even be the same for some courses, especially for colleges and universities offering standard ones at unusual times. But for nontraditional programs, students may also pay fees for services such as credit or transcript review, evaluation, advisement, and portfolio assessment.

Students are also responsible for postage and handling or setup expenses for independent study courses, as well as for all examination and transcript fees for transferring credits. Usually, the more nontraditional the program, the more detailed the fees. Some schools charge a yearly enrollment fee rather than tuition for degree completion candidates who want their files to remain active.

Although tuition and fees might seem expensive, most educators tell you not to let money come between you and your educational goals. Talk to someone in the financial aid department of the school you plan to attend or check your library for publications about financial aid sources. The U.S. Department of Education publishes a guide to Federal aid programs such as Pell Grants, student loans, and work-study. To order the free 74-page booklet, *The Student Guide: Financial Aid from the U.S. Department of Education,* contact:

Federal Student Aid Information Center
P.O. Box 84
Washington, DC 20044
1 (800) 4FED-AID (433-3243)

Resources

Information on how to earn a high school diploma or college degree without following the usual routes is available from several organizations and in numerous publications. Information on nontraditional graduate degree programs, available for master's through doctoral level, though not discussed in this article, can usually be obtained from the same resources that detail bachelor's degree programs.

National Learning Corporation publishes study guides for all of these exams, for both general examinations and tests in specific subject areas. To order study guides, or to browse their catalog featuring more than 5,000 titles, visit NLC online at www.passbooks.com, or contact them by phone at (800) 632-8888.

Organizations

Adult learners should always contact their local school system, community college, or university to learn about programs that are readily available. The following national organizations can also supply information:

American Council on Education
One Dupont Circle
Washington, DC 20036-1193
(202) 939-9300

Within the American Council on Education, the Center for Adult Learning and Educational Credentials administers the National External Diploma Program, the GED Program, the Program on Noncollegiate Sponsored Instruction, the Credit by Examination Program, and the Military Evaluations Program.

DANTES Subject Standardized Tests

INTRODUCTION

The DANTES (Defense Activity for Non-Traditional Education Support) subject standardized tests are comprehensive college and graduate level examinations given by the Armed Forces, colleges and graduate schools as end-of-subject course evaluation final examinations or to obtain college equivalency credits in the various subject areas tested.

The DANTES Examination Program enables students to obtain college credit for what they have learned on the job, through self-study, personal interest, correspondence courses or by any other means. It is used by colleges and universities to award college credit to students who demonstrate that they know as much as students completing an equivalent college course. It is a cost-efficient, time-saving way for students to use their knowledge to accomplish their educational goals.

Most schools accept the American Council on Education (ACE) recommendations for the minimum score required and the amount of credit awarded, but not all schools do. Be sure to check the policy regarding the score level required for credit and the number of credits to be awarded.

Not all tests are accepted by all institutions. Even when a test is accepted by an institution, it may not be acceptable for every program at that institution. Before considering testing, ascertain the acceptability of a specific test for a particular course.

Colleges and universities that administer DANTES tests may administer them to any applicant – or they may administer the tests only to students registered at their institution. Decisions about who will be allowed to test are made by the school. Students should contact the test center to determine current policies and schedules for DANTES testing.

Colleges and universities authorized to administer DANTES tests usually do so throughout the calendar year. Each school sets its own fee for test administration and establishes its own testing schedule. Contact the representative at the administering school directly to make arrangements for testing.

Checklist
For Students

✓ Visit **www.getcollegecredit.com** to obtain a list of tests, fact sheets, test preparation materials, participating colleges and universities, and much more.

✓ Contact your school advisor to confirm that the DSST you selected will fit into your curriculum.

✓ Consult the ***DSST Candidate Information Bulletin*** for answers to specific questions.

✓ Contact the test site to schedule your test.

✓ Prepare for your examination by using the fact sheet as a guide.

✓ Take the test.

If you would like a score report sent to your college or university, it is a good idea to bring the four-digit code with you. You must write the DSST Test Center Code for that institution on your answer sheet at the time of testing. DSST Test Center Codes are noted in the DSST Participating Colleges and Universities listing on the Web site.

If you prefer to send a score report to an institution at a later date, there is a transcript fee of $20 for each transcript ordered.

Thomson Prometric
DSST Program
2000 Lenox Drive, Third Floor
Lawrenceville, NJ 08648

Toll-free: 877-471-9860
609-895-5011

E-mail: pnj-dsst@thomson.com

MAKING A COLLEGE DEGREE WITHIN YOUR REACH

Today, there are many educational alternatives to the classroom—you can learn from your job, your reading, your independent study, and special interests you pursue. You may already have learned the subject matter covered by some college-level courses.

The DSST Program is a nationally recognized testing program that gives you the opportunity to receive college credit for learning acquired outside the traditional college classroom. Colleges and universities throughout the United States administer the program, developed by Thomson Prometric, year-round. Annually, over 90,000 DSSTs are administered to individuals who are interested in continuing their education. Take advantage of the DSST testing program; it speeds the educational process and provides the flexibility adults need, making earning a degree more feasible.

Since requirements differ from college to college, please check with the credit-awarding institution before taking a DSST. More than 1,800 colleges and universities currently award credit for DSSTs, and the number is growing every day. You can choose from 37 test titles in the areas of Social Science, Business, Mathematics, Applied Technology, Humanities, and Physical Science. A brief description of each examination is found on the pages that follow.

Reach Your Career Goals Through DSSTs

Use DSSTs to help you earn your degree, get a promotion, or simply demonstrate that you have college-level knowledge in subjects relevant to your work.

Save Time...

You don't have to sit through classes when you have previously acquired the knowledge or experience for most of what is being taught and can learn the rest yourself. You might be able to bypass introductory-level courses in subject areas you already know.

Save Money...

DSSTs save you money because the classes you bypass by earning credit through the DSST Program are classes you won't have to pay for on your way to earning your degree. You can use the money instead to take more advanced courses that can be more challenging and rewarding.

Improve Your Chances for Admission to College

Each college has its own admission policies; however, having passing scores for DSSTs on your transcript can provide strong evidence of how well you can perform at the college level.

Gain Confidence Performing at a College Level

Many adults returning to college find that lack of confidence is often the greatest hurdle to overcome. Passing a DSST demonstrates your ability to perform on a college level.

Make Up for Courses You May Have Missed

You may be ready to graduate from college and find that you are a few credits short of earning your degree. By using semester breaks, vacation time, or leisure time to study independently, you can prepare to take one or more DSSTs, fulfill your academic requirements, and graduate on time.

If You Cannot Attend Regularly Scheduled Classes...

If your lifestyle or responsibilities prevent you from attending regularly scheduled classes, you can earn your college degree from a college offering an external degree program. The DSST Program allows you to earn your degree by study and experience outside the traditional classroom.

Many colleges and universities offer external degree or distance learning programs. For additional information, contact the college you plan to attend or:

Center for Lifelong Learning
American Council on Education
One DuPont Circle NW, Suite 250
Washington, DC 20036
202-939-9475
www.acenet.edu
(Select "Center for Lifelong Learning" under "Programs & Services"
for more information)

Fact Sheets

For each test, there is a Fact Sheet that outlines the topics covered by each test and includes a list of sample questions, a list of recommended references of books that would be useful for review, and the number of credits awarded for a passing score as recommended by the American Council on Education (ACE). *Please note that some schools require scores that are higher than the minimum ACE-recommended passing score.* It is suggested that you check with your college or university to determine what score they require in order to earn credit. You can obtain Fact Sheets by:

- Downloading them from www.getcollegecredit.com
- E-mailing a request to pnj-dsst@thomson.com
- Completing a Candidate Publications Order Form

DSST Online Practice Tests

DSST online practice tests contain items that reflect a *partial range of difficulty* identified in the Content Outline section on each Fact Sheet. There is an online DSST Practice Test in the following categories:

- Mathematics
- Social Science
- Business
- Physical Science
- Applied Technology
- Humanities

Although the online DSST Practice Test questions do not indicate the full range of difficulty you would find in an actual DSST test, they will help you assess your knowledge level. Each online DSST Practice Test can be purchased by visiting www.getcollegecredit.com and clicking on DSST Practice Exams.

TAKING DSST EXAMINATIONS

Earning College Credit for DSST Examinations

To find out if the college of your choice awards credit for passing DSST scores, contact the admissions office or counseling and testing office. The college can also provide information on the scores required for awarding credit, the number of credit hours awarded, and any courses that can be bypassed with satisfactory scores.

It is important that you contact the institution of your choice as early as possible since credit-awarding policies differ among colleges and universities.

Where to Take DSSTs

DSSTs are administered at colleges and universities nationwide. Each location determines the frequency and scheduling of test administrations. To obtain the most current list of participating DSST colleges and universities:
- Visit and download the information from www.getcollegecredit.com
- E-mail pnj-dsst@thomson.com

Scheduling Your Examination

Please be aware that some colleges and universities provide DSST testing services to enrolled students only. After you have selected a college or university that administers DSSTs, you will need to contact them to schedule your test date.

The fee to take a DSST is $60 per test. This fee entitles you to two score reports after the test is scored. One will be sent directly to you and the other will be sent to the college or university that you designate on your answer sheet. You may pay the test fee with a certified check or U.S. money order made payable to Thomson Prometric or you may charge the test fee to your Visa, MasterCard or American Express credit card. Note: The credit card statement will reflect a charge from Thomson Prometric for all DSST examinations. *(Declined credit card charges will be assessed an additional $25 processing fee.)*

In addition, the test site may also require a test administration fee for each examination, to be paid directly to the institution. Contact the test site to determine its administration fee and payment policy.

Other Testing Arrangements

If you are unable to find a participating DSST college or university in your area, you may want to contact the testing office of a local accredited college or university to determine whether a representative from that office will agree to administer the test(s) for you.

The school's representative should then contact the DSST Program at 866-794-3497 to arrange for this administration. If you are unable to locate a test site, contact Thomson Prometric for assistance at pnj-dsst@thomson.com or 866-794-3497.

Testing Accommodations for Students with Disabilities

Thomson Prometric is committed to serving test takers with disabilities by providing services and reasonable testing accommodations as set forth in the provisions of the *Americans with Disabilities Act* (ADA). If you have a disability, as prescribed by the ADA, and require special testing services or arrangements, please contact the test administrator at the test site. You will be asked to submit to the test administrator documentation of your disability and your request for special accommodations. The test administrator will then forward your documentation along with your request for testing accommodations to Thomson Prometric for approval.

Please submit your request as far in advance of your test date as possible so that the necessary accommodations can be made. Only test takers with documented disabilities are eligible for special accommodations.

On the Day of the Examination
It is important to review this information and to have the correct identification present on the day of the examination:
- Arrive on time as a courtesy to the test administrator.
- Bring a valid form of government-issued identification that includes a current photo and your signature (acceptable documents include a driver's license, passport, state-issued identification card or military identification). *Anyone who fails to present valid identification will not be allowed to test.*
- Bring several No. 2 (soft-lead) sharpened pencils with good erasers, a watch, and a black pen if you will be writing an essay.
- Do not bring books or papers.
- Do not bring an alarm watch that beeps, a telephone, or a phone beeper into the testing room.
- The use of nonprogrammable calculators, slide rules, scratch paper and/or other materials is permitted for some of the tests.

DSST SCORING POLICIES

Your DSST examination scores are reported only to you, unless you request that they be sent elsewhere. If you want your scores sent to your college, you must provide the correct DSST code number of the school on your answer sheet at the time you take the test. See the *DSST Directory of Colleges and Universities* on the Web site www.getcollegecredit.com.

If your institution is not listed, contact Thomson Prometric at 866-794-3497 to establish a code number. (Some schools may require a student to be enrolled prior to receiving a score report.)

Receiving Your Score Report
Allow approximately four weeks after testing to receive your score report.
Calling DSST Customer Service before the required four-week score processing time has elapsed will not expedite the processing of your scores. Due to privacy and security requirements, scores will not be reported to students over the telephone under any circumstance.

Scoring of Principles of Public Speaking Speeches
The speech portion of the *Principles of Public Speaking* examination will be sent to speech raters who are faculty members at accredited colleges that currently teach or have previously taught the course. Scores for the *Principles of Public Speaking* examination are available six to eight weeks from receipt by Thomson Prometric. If you take the *Principles of Public Speaking* examination and fail (either the objective, speech portion, or both), you must follow the retesting policy waiting period of six months (180 days) before retaking the entire exam.

Essays

The essays for *Ethics in America* and *Technical Writing* are <u>optional</u> and thus are not scored by raters. The essays are forwarded to the college or university that you designate, along with your score report, for their use in determining the award of credit. <u>Before taking the *Ethics in America* or *Technical Writing* examinations, check with your college or university to determine whether the essay is required.</u>

NOTE: *Principles of Public Speaking* speech topic cassette tapes and essays are kept on file at Thomson Prometric for one year from the date of administration.

How to Get Transcripts

There is a $20 fee for each transcript you request. Payment must be in the form of a certified check, U.S. money order payable to Thomson Prometric, or credit card. Personal checks and debit cards are NOT an acceptable method of payment. One transcript may include scores for one or more examinations taken. To request a transcript, download the Transcript Order Form from www.getcollegecredit.com.

DESCRIPTION OF THE DSST EXAMINATIONS

Mathematics

• **Fundamentals of College Algebra** covers mathematical concepts such as fundamental algebraic operations; linear, absolute value; quadratic equations, inequalities, radials, exponents and logarithms, factoring polynomials and graphing. The use of a nonprogrammable, handheld calculator is permitted.

• **Principles of Statistics** tests the understanding of the various topics of statistics, both qualitatively and quantitatively, and the ability to apply statistical methods to solve a variety of problems. The topics included in this test are descriptive statistics; correlation and regression; probability; chance models and sampling and tests of significance. The use of a nonprogrammable, handheld calculator is permitted.

Social Science

• **Art of the Western World** deals with the history of art during the following periods: classical; Romanesque and Gothic; early Renaissance; high Renaissance, Baroque; rococo; neoclassicism and romanticism; realism, impressionism and post-impressionism; early twentieth century; and post-World War II.

• **Western Europe Since 1945** tests the knowledge of basic facts and terms and the understanding of concepts and principles related to the areas of the historical background of the aftermath of the Second World War and rebuilding of Europe; national political systems; issues and policies in Western European societies; European institutions and processes; and Europe's relations with the rest of the world.

• **An Introduction to the Modern Middle East** emphasizes core knowledge (including geography, Judaism, Christianity, Islam, ethnicity); nineteenth-century European impact; twentieth-century Western influences; World Wars I and II; new nations; social and cultural changes (1900-1960) and the Middle East from 1960 to present.

• **Human/Cultural Geography** includes the Earth and basic facts (coordinate systems, maps, physiography, atmosphere, soils and vegetation, water); culture and environment, spatial processes (social processes, modern economic systems, settlement patterns, political geography); and regional geography.

- **Rise and Fall of the Soviet Union** covers Russia under the Old Regime; the Revolutionary Period; New Economic Policy; Pre-war Stalinism; The Second World War; Post-war Stalinism; The Khrushchev Years; The Brezhnev Era; and reform and collapse.

- **A History of the Vietnam War** covers the history of the roots of the Vietnam War; the First Vietnam War (1946-1954); pre-war developments (1954-1963); American involvement in the Vietnam War; Tet (1968); Vietnamizing the War (1968-1973); Cambodia and Laos; peace; legacies and lessons.

- **The Civil War and Reconstruction** covers the Civil War from presecession (1861) through Reconstruction. It includes causes of the war; secession; Fort Sumter; the war in the east and in the west; major battles; the political situation; assassination of Lincoln; end of the Confederacy; and Reconstruction.

- **Foundations of Education** includes topics such as contemporary issues in education; past and current influences on education (philosophies, democratic ideals, social/economic influences); and the interrelationships between contemporary issues and influences.

- **Life-span Developmental Psychology** covers models and theories; methods of study; ethical issues; biological development; perception, learning and memory; cognition and language; social, emotional, and personality development; social behaviors, family life cycle, extrafamilial settings; singlehood and cohabitation; occupational development and retirement; adjustment to life stresses; and bereavement and loss.

- **Drug and Alcohol Abuse** includes such topics as drug use in society; classification of drugs; pharmacological principles; alcohol (types, effects of, alcoholism); general principles and use of sedative hypnotics, narcotic analgesics, stimulants, and hallucinogens; other drugs (inhalants, steroids); and prevention/treatment.

- **General Anthropology** deals with anthropology as a discipline; theoretical perspectives; physical anthropology; archaeology; social organization; economic organization; political organization; religion; and modernization and application of anthropology.

- **Introduction to Law Enforcement** includes topics such as history and professional movement of law enforcement; overview of the U.S. criminal justice system; police systems in the U.S.; police organization, management, and issues; and U.S. law and precedents.

- **Criminal Justice** deals with criminal behavior (crime in the U.S., theories of crime, types of crime); the criminal justice system (historical origins, legal foundations, due process); police; the court system (history and organization, adult court system, juvenile court, pre-trial and post-trial processes); and corrections.

- **Fundamentals of Counseling** covers historical development (significant influences and people); counselor roles and functions; the counseling relationship; and theoretical approaches to counseling.

Business
- **Principles of Finance** deals with financial statements and planning; time value of money; working capital management; valuation and characteristics; capital budgeting; cost of capital; risk and return; and international financial management. The use of a nonprogrammable, handheld calculator is permitted.

- **Principles of Financial Accounting** includes topics such as general concepts and principles, accounting cycle and classification; transaction analysis; accruals and deferrals; cash and internal control; current accounts; long- and short-term liabilities; capital stock; and financial statements. The use of a nonprogrammable, handheld calculator is permitted.

- **Human Resource Management** covers general employment issues; job analysis; training and development; performance appraisals; compensation issues; security issues; personnel legislation and regulation; labor relations and current issues; an overview of the Human Resource Management Field; Human Resource Planning; Staffing; training and development; compensation issues; safety and health; employee rights and discipline; employment law; labor relations and current issues and trends.

- **Organizational Behavior** deals with the study of organizational behavior (scientific approaches, research designs, data collection methods); individual processes and characteristics; interpersonal and group processes and characteristics; organizational processes and characteristics; and change and development processes.

- **Principles of Supervision** deals with the roles and responsibilities of the supervisor; management functions (planning, organization and staffing, directing at the supervisory level); and other topics (legal issues, stress management, union environments, quality concerns).

- **Business Law II** covers topics such as sales of goods; debtor and creditor relations; business organizations; property; and commercial paper.

- **Introduction to Computing** includes topics such as history and technological generations; hardware/software; applications to information technology; program development; data management; communications and connectivity; and computing and society. The use of a nonprogrammable, handheld calculator is permitted.

- **Management Information Systems** covers systems theory, analysis and design of systems, hardware and software; database management; telecommunications; management of the MIS functional area and informational support.

- **Introduction to Business** deals with economic issues affecting business; international business; government and business; forms of business ownership; small business, entrepreneurship and franchise; management process; human resource management; production and operations; marketing management; financial management; risk management and insurance; and management and information systems.

- **Money and Banking** covers the role and kinds of money; commercial banks and other financial intermediaries; central banking and the Federal Reserve system; money and macroeconomics activity; monetary policy in the U.S.; and the international monetary system.

- **Personal Finance** includes topics such as financial goals and values; budgeting; credit and debt; major purchases; taxes; insurance; investments; and retirement and estate planning. The use of auxiliary materials, such as calculators and slide rules, is NOT permitted.

- **Business Mathematics** deals with basic operations with integers, fractions, and decimals; round numbers; ratios; averages; business graphs; simple interest; compound interest and annuities; net pay and deductions; discounts and markups; depreciation and net worth; corporate securities; distribution of ownership; and stock and asset turnover.

Physical Science
• **Astronomy** covers the history of astronomy, celestial mechanics; celestial systems; astronomical instruments; the solar system; nature and evolution; the galaxy; the universe; determining astronomical distances; and life in the universe.

• **Here's to Your Health** covers mental health and behavior; human development and relationships; substance abuse; fitness and nutrition; risk factors, disease, and disease prevention; and safety, consumer awareness, and environmental concerns.

• **Environment and Humanity** deals with topics such as ecological concepts (ecosystems, global ecology, food chains and webs); environmental impacts; environmental management and conservation; and political processes and the future.

• **Principles of Physical Science I** includes physics: Newton's Laws of Motion; energy and momentum; thermodynamics; wave and optics; electricity and magnetism; chemistry: properties of matter; atomic theory and structure; and chemical reactions.

• **Physical Geology** covers Earth materials; igneous, sedimentary, and metamorphic rocks; surface processes (weathering, groundwater, glaciers, oceanic systems, deserts and winds, hydrologic cycle); internal Earth processes; and applications (mineral and energy resources, environmental geology).

Applied Technology
• **Technical Writing** covers topics such as theory and practice of technical writing; purpose, content, and organizational patterns of common types of technical documents; elements of various technical reports; and technical editing. Students have the option to write a short essay on one of the technical topics provided. Thomson Prometric will not score the essay; however, for determining the award of credit, a copy of the essay will be forwarded to the college or university you've designated along with the score report or transcript.

Humanities
• **Ethics in America** deals with ethical traditions (Greek views, Biblical traditions, moral law, consequential ethics, feminist ethics); ethical analysis of issues arising in interpersonal and personal-societal relationships and in professional and occupational roles; and relationships between ethical traditions and the ethical analysis of situations. Students have the option to write an essay to analyze a morally problematic situation in terms of issues relevant to a decision and arguments for alternative positions. Thomson Prometric will not score the essay; however, for determining the award of credit, a copy of the essay will be forwarded to the college or university you've designated along with the score report or transcript.

• **Introduction to World Religions** covers topics such as dimensions and approaches to religion; primal religions; Hinduism; Buddhism; Confucianism; Taoism; Judaism; Christianity; and Islam.

• **Principles of Public Speaking** consists of two parts: Part One consists of multiple-choice questions covering considerations of Principles of Public Speaking; audience analysis; purposes of speeches; structure/organization; content/supporting materials; research; language and style; delivery; communication apprehension; listening and feedback; and criticism and evaluation. Part Two requires the student to record an impromptu persuasive speech that will be scored.

FREQUENTLY ASKED QUESTIONS ABOUT DSSTs

In order to pass the test, must I study from one of the recommended references?

The recommended references are a listing of books that were being used as textbooks in college courses of the same or similar title at the time the test was developed. Appropriate textbooks for study are not limited to those listed in the fact sheet. If you wish to obtain study resources to prepare for the examination, you may reference either the current edition of the listed titles or textbooks currently used at a local college or university for the same class title. It is recommended that you reference more than one textbook on the topics outlined in the fact sheet. You should begin by checking textbook content against the content outline included on the front page of the DSST fact sheet before selecting textbooks that cover the text content from which to study. Textbooks may be found at the campus bookstore of a local college or university offering a course on the subject.

Is there a penalty for guessing on the tests?

There is no penalty for guessing on DSSTs, so you should mark an answer for each question.

How much time will I have to complete the test?

Many DSSTs can be completed within 90 minutes; however, additional time can be allowed if necessary.

What should I do if I find a test question irregularity?

Continue testing and then report the irregularity to the test administrator after the test. This may be done by asking that the test administrator note the irregularity on the Supervisor's Irregularity Report or you can write to Thomson Prometric, DSST Program, 2000 Lenox Drive, Third Floor, Lawrenceville, NJ 08648, and indicate the form and question number(s) or circumstances as well as your name and address.

When will I receive my score report?

Allow approximately four weeks from the date of testing to receive your score report. Allow six to eight weeks to receive a score report for the *Principles of Public Speaking* examination.

Will my test scores be released without my permission?

Your test score will not be released to anyone other than the school you designate on your answer sheet unless you write to us and ask us to send a transcript elsewhere. Instructions about how to do this can be found on your score report. Your scores may be used for research purposes, but individual scores are never made public nor are individuals identified if research findings are made public.

If I do not achieve a passing score on the test, how long must I wait until I can take the test again?

If you do not receive a score on the test that will enable you to obtain credit for the course, you may take the test again after six months (180 days). Please do not attempt to take the test before six months (180 days) have passed because you will receive a score report marked *invalid* and your test fee will not be refunded.

Can my test scores be canceled?

The test administrator is required to report any irregularities to Thomson Prometric. <u>The consequence of bringing unauthorized materials into the testing room, or giving or receiving help, will be the forfeiture of your test fee and the invalidation of test scores.</u> The DSST Program reserves the right to cancel scores and not issue score reports in such situations.

What can I do if I feel that my test scores were not accurately reported?

Thomson Prometric recognizes the extreme importance of test results to candidates and has a multi-step quality-control procedure to help ensure that reported scores are accurate. If you have reason to believe that your score(s) were not accurately reported, you may request to have your answer sheet reviewed and hand scored.

The fees for this service are:
- $20 fee if requested within six months of the test date
- $30 fee if requested more than six months from the test date
- $30 fee if a re-evaluation of the *Principles of Public Speaking* speech is requested

The fee for this service can be paid by credit card or by certified check or U.S. money order payable to Thomson Prometric. Submit your request for score verification along with the appropriate fee or credit card information (credit card number and expiration date) to Thomson Prometric, DSST Program, 2000 Lenox Drive, Third Floor, Lawrenceville, NJ 08648. Include your full name, the test title, the date you took the test, and your Social Security number. Candidates will be notified if a scoring discrepancy is discovered within four weeks of receipt of the request.

What does ACE recommendation mean?

The ACE recommendation is the minimum passing score recommended by the American Council on Education for any given test. It is equivalent to the average score of students in the DSST norming sample who received a grade of C for the course. Some schools require a score higher than the ACE recommendation.

Who is NLC?

National Learning Corporation (NLC) has been successfully preparing candidates for 40 years for over 5,000 exams. NLC publishes Passbook® study guides to help candidates prepare for all DANTES and CLEP exams and almost every other type of exam from high school through adult career.

Go to our website — www.passbooks.com — or call (800) 632-8888 for information about ordering our Passbooks.

To get detailed information on the DSST program and DSST preparation materials, visit www.getcollegecredit.com.

If you are interested in taking the DSST exams, call 877-471-9860 or e-mail pnj-dsst@thomson.com.

Fact Sheet

ASTRONOMY

TEST INFORMATION

This test was developed to enable schools to award credit to students for knowledge equivalent to that, which is learned, by students taking the course. The school may choose to award college credit to the student based on the achievement of a passing score. The passing score for each examination is determined by the school based on recommendations from the American Council on Education (ACE). This minimum credit-awarding score is equal to the mean score of students in the norming sample who received a grade of C in the course. Some schools set their own standards for awarding credit and may require a higher score than the ACE recommendation. Students should obtain this information from the institution where they expect to receive credit.

CONTENT

The following topics, which are commonly taught in courses on this subject, are covered by this examination.

		Approximate Percent
I.	History of Astronomy A. Nature of science B. How scientists think and work	9%
II.	Celestial Mechanics, Including Gravitation and Relativity	5%
III.	Celestial Systems A. Earth and the sky B. Earth and the Moon C. Time and the calendar	13%
IV.	Astronomical Instruments A. Measurement and analysis of starlight B. The electromagnetic spectrum	12%
V.	The Solar System A. Contents, form, and motions B. Evolution	19%
VI.	The Sun and Stars: Nature and Evolution	17%
VII.	Our Galaxy: Contents and Structure	7%
VIII.	The Universe: Contents, Structure, and Evolution	10%
IX.	Determining Astronomical Distances	5%
X.	Life in the Universe	3%

Questions on the test require candidates to demonstrate the following abilities. Some questions may require more than one of the abilities.

- Knowledge of basic facts and terms
  (about 45 - 50% of the examination)

- Understanding of concepts and principles
  (about 40 - 45% of the examination)

- Ability to apply knowledge to specific cases or issues
  (about 5 - 10% of the examination)

From the official announcement for educational purposes

SAMPLE QUESTIONS

1. In the northern hemisphere, the vernal equinox is the position occupied by the Sun on the first day of

    (A) summer
    (B) fall
    (C) spring
    (D) winter

2. Which of the following is the best illustration of Newton's third law?

    (A) A skater coasting across the ice
    (B) The spinning of a top
    (C) The swinging of a pendulum
    (D) The recoil of a shotgun

3. The energy in the interior of a white dwarf is transported outward in the same fashion as the energy is transmitted

    (A) in an airplane shockwave
    (B) from an electric oven
    (C) from a hot-air furnace
    (D) from tip to handle of a hot poker

4. The most important advantage of a large telescope aperture is that it

    (A) allows a large amount of radiation to be collected
    (B) gives a higher magnification of the objects observed
    (C) is less affected by the trembling of the Earth's atmosphere
    (D) produces a larger diffraction ring when distant stars are observed

5. Which of the following statements is true about the steady-state cosmology?

    (A) It explains the isotropic nature of the remnant radiation from a giant fireball.
    (B) It appears to violate the law of conservation of matter in empty space.
    (C) It predicts a negative value for the Hubble Constant.
    (D) It explains the galactic red shifts as gravitational effects.

6. Where is the Moon when there are spring tides on Earth?

    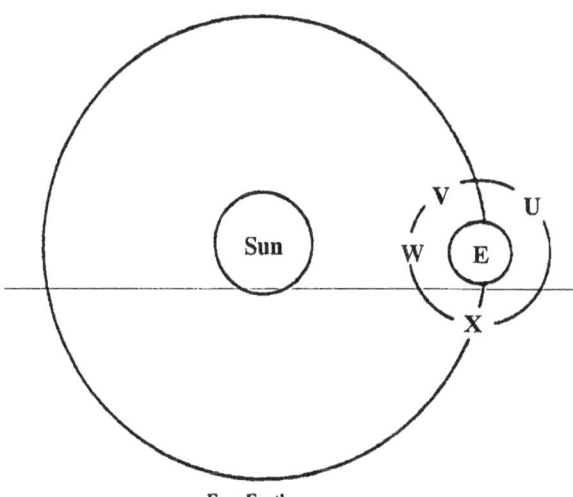

    E = Earth
    U, V, W, X = Positions of the Moon

    (A) U
    (B) V
    (C) W
    (D) X

7. The bending of rays of light as they pass from one transparent medium into another is called

    (A) reflection
    (B) diffraction
    (C) dispersion
    (D) refraction

8. Which of the following planets has been observed to have extensive Van Allen belts similar to those of Earth?

    (A) Mercury
    (B) Mars
    (C) Jupiter
    (D) Venus

9. The fact that most stars observed are on the Main Sequence implies that a star spends the greatest proportion of its lifetime

    (A) contracting to reach the Main Sequence
    (B) as a giant off the Main Sequence
    (C) expanding to reach the Main Sequence
    (D) on the Main Sequence

10. At the present time in the Sun's lifetime, the major source of the Sun's energy lies in

    (A) electron-proton collisions
    (B) gravitational contraction
    (C) nuclear fusion
    (D) matter-antimatter annihilation

11. The Universe as we know it began its existence as a hot, dense cloud of matter and radiation approximately how many years ago?

    (A) 5 billion
    (B) 15 billion
    (C) 50 billion
    (D) 100 billion

STUDYING FOR THE EXAMINATION

The following is a list of reference publications that were being used as textbooks in college courses of the same or similar title at the time the test was developed. Appropriate textbooks for study are not limited to those listed below. If you wish to obtain study resources to prepare for the examination, you may reference either the current edition of the following titles **or** textbooks currently used at a local college or university for the same class title. It is recommended that you reference **more than one textbook** on the topics outlined in this fact sheet. You should **begin by checking textbook content against the content outline** included on the front page of this Fact Sheet **before** selecting textbooks that cover the test content from which to study. Textbooks may be found at the campus bookstore of a local college or university offering a course on the subject.

Sources for study material suggested but not limited to the following:

Abell, George *Exploration of the Universe*. New York: CBS/Saunders College Publishing, current edition.

Jastrow, Robert, and Malcolm H. Thompson. *Astronomy: Fundamentals and Frontiers*. New York: John Wiley and Sons, Inc., current edition.

Kaufmann, William J. *Discovering the Universe*. New York: Freeman, current edition.

Pasachoff, Jay M. *Astronomy: From Earth to the Universe*. Philadelphia: Saunders College Publishing, current edition.

Seeds, Michael. *Horizons: Exploring the Universe*. Belmont, CA: Wadsworth, current edition.

Zeilik, Michael. *Astronomy: The Evolving Universe*. New York: John Wiley and Sons, Inc., current edition.

Current textbook used by a local college or university for a course on the subject.

CREDIT RECOMMENDATIONS

The Center for Adult Learning and Educational Credentials of the American Council on Education (ACE) has reviewed and evaluated the DSST test development process and has made the following recommendations:

Area or Course Equivalent: Astronomy
Level: Lower-Level Baccalaureate
Amount of Credit: Three (3) semester hours
Source: ACE Commission on Educational Credit and Credentials

INFORMATION

Colleges and universities that would like additional information about the national norming, or assistance in local norming or score validation studies should write to: DSST Program, Prometric, 2000 Lenox Drive, 3rd Floor, Lawrenceville, NJ 08648.

It is advisable that schools develop a consistent policy about awarding credit based on scores from this test and that the policy be reviewed periodically. Prometric will be happy to help schools in this effort.

Correct Responses to sample questions: 1．C; 2．D; 3．D; 4．A; 5．B; 6．C; 7．D; 8．C; 9．D; 10．C; 11．B.

HOW TO TAKE A TEST

You have studied long, hard and conscientiously.

With your official admission card in hand, and your heart pounding, you have been admitted to the examination room.

You note that there are several hundred other applicants in the examination room waiting to take the same test.

They all appear to be equally well prepared.

You know that nothing but your best effort will suffice. The "moment of truth" is at hand: you now have to demonstrate objectively, in writing, your knowledge of content and your understanding of subject matter.

You are fighting the most important battle of your life—to pass and/or score high on an examination which will determine your career and provide the economic basis for your livelihood.

What extra, special things should you know and should you do in taking the examination?

I. YOU MUST PASS AN EXAMINATION

A. WHAT EVERY CANDIDATE SHOULD KNOW
　　Examination applicants often ask us for help in preparing for the written test. What can I study in advance? What kinds of questions will be asked? How will the test be given? How will the papers be graded?

B. HOW ARE EXAMS DEVELOPED?
　　Examinations are carefully written by trained technicians who are specialists in the field known as "psychological measurement," in consultation with recognized authorities in the field of work that the test will cover. These experts recommend the subject matter areas or skills to be tested; only those knowledges or skills important to your success on the job are included. The most reliable books and source materials available are used as references. Together, the experts and technicians judge the difficulty level of the questions.
　　Test technicians know how to phrase questions so that the problem is clearly stated. Their ethics do not permit "trick" or "catch" questions. Questions may have been tried out on sample groups, or subjected to statistical analysis, to determine their usefulness.
　　Written tests are often used in combination with performance tests, ratings of training and experience, and oral interviews. All of these measures combine to form the best-known means of finding the right person for the right job.

II. HOW TO PASS THE WRITTEN TEST

A. BASIC STEPS

1) Study the announcement

How, then, can you know what subjects to study? Our best answer is: "Learn as much as possible about the class of positions for which you've applied." The exam will test the knowledge, skills and abilities needed to do the work.

Your most valuable source of information about the position you want is the official exam announcement. This announcement lists the training and experience qualifications. Check these standards and apply only if you come reasonably close to meeting them. Many jurisdictions preview the written test in the exam announcement by including a section called "Knowledge and Abilities Required," "Scope of the Examination," or some similar heading. Here you will find out specifically what fields will be tested.

2) Choose appropriate study materials

If the position for which you are applying is technical or advanced, you will read more advanced, specialized material. If you are already familiar with the basic principles of your field, elementary textbooks would waste your time. Concentrate on advanced textbooks and technical periodicals. Think through the concepts and review difficult problems in your field.

These are all general sources. You can get more ideas on your own initiative, following these leads. For example, training manuals and publications of the government agency which employs workers in your field can be useful, particularly for technical and professional positions. A letter or visit to the government department involved may result in more specific study suggestions, and certainly will provide you with a more definite idea of the exact nature of the position you are seeking.

3) Study this book!

III. KINDS OF TESTS

Tests are used for purposes other than measuring knowledge and ability to perform specified duties. For some positions, it is equally important to test ability to make adjustments to new situations or to profit from training. In others, basic mental abilities not dependent on information are essential. Questions which test these things may not appear as pertinent to the duties of the position as those which test for knowledge and information. Yet they are often highly important parts of a fair examination. For very general questions, it is almost impossible to help you direct your study efforts. What we can do is to point out some of the more common of these general abilities needed in public service positions and describe some typical questions.

1) General information

Broad, general information has been found useful for predicting job success in some kinds of work. This is tested in a variety of ways, from vocabulary lists to questions about current events. Basic background in some field of work, such as sociology or economics, may be sampled in a group of questions. Often these are principles which have become familiar to most persons through exposure rather than through formal training. It is difficult to advise you how to study for these questions; being alert to the world around you is our best suggestion.

2) Verbal ability

An example of an ability needed in many positions is verbal or language ability. Verbal ability is, in brief, the ability to use and understand words. Vocabulary and grammar tests are typical measures of this ability. Reading comprehension or paragraph interpretation questions are common in many kinds of civil service tests. You are given a paragraph of written material and asked to find its central meaning.

IV. KINDS OF QUESTIONS

1. Multiple-choice Questions

Most popular of the short-answer questions is the "multiple choice" or "best answer" question. It can be used, for example, to test for factual knowledge, ability to solve problems or judgment in meeting situations found at work.

A multiple-choice question is normally one of three types:
- It can begin with an incomplete statement followed by several possible endings. You are to find the one ending which best completes the statement, although some of the others may not be entirely wrong.
- It can also be a complete statement in the form of a question which is answered by choosing one of the statements listed.
- It can be in the form of a problem – again you select the best answer.

Here is an example of a multiple-choice question with a discussion which should give you some clues as to the method for choosing the right answer:

When an employee has a complaint about his assignment, the action which will best help him overcome his difficulty is to
- A. discuss his difficulty with his coworkers
- B. take the problem to the head of the organization
- C. take the problem to the person who gave him the assignment
- D. say nothing to anyone about his complaint

In answering this question, you should study each of the choices to find which is best. Consider choice "A" – Certainly an employee may discuss his complaint with fellow employees, but no change or improvement can result, and the complaint remains unresolved. Choice "B" is a poor choice since the head of the organization probably does not know what assignment you have been given, and taking your problem to him is known as "going over the head" of the supervisor. The supervisor, or person who made the assignment, is the person who can clarify it or correct any injustice. Choice "C" is, therefore, correct. To say nothing, as in choice "D," is unwise. Supervisors have and interest in knowing the problems employees are facing, and the employee is seeking a solution to his problem.

2. True/False

3. Matching Questions

Matching an answer from a column of choices within another column.

V. RECORDING YOUR ANSWERS

Computer terminals are used more and more today for many different kinds of exams.

For an examination with very few applicants, you may be told to record your answers in the test booklet itself. Separate answer sheets are much more common. If this separate answer sheet is to be scored by machine – and this is often the case – it is highly important that you mark your answers correctly in order to get credit.

VI. BEFORE THE TEST

YOUR PHYSICAL CONDITION IS IMPORTANT

If you are not well, you can't do your best work on tests. If you are half asleep, you can't do your best either. Here are some tips:

1) Get about the same amount of sleep you usually get. Don't stay up all night before the test, either partying or worrying—DON'T DO IT!
2) If you wear glasses, be sure to wear them when you go to take the test. This goes for hearing aids, too.
3) If you have any physical problems that may keep you from doing your best, be sure to tell the person giving the test. If you are sick or in poor health, you relay cannot do your best on any test. You can always come back and take the test some other time.

Common sense will help you find procedures to follow to get ready for an examination. Too many of us, however, overlook these sensible measures. Indeed, nervousness and fatigue have been found to be the most serious reasons why applicants fail to do their best on civil service tests. Here is a list of reminders:

- Begin your preparation early – Don't wait until the last minute to go scurrying around for books and materials or to find out what the position is all about.
- Prepare continuously – An hour a night for a week is better than an all-night cram session. This has been definitely established. What is more, a night a week for a month will return better dividends than crowding your study into a shorter period of time.
- Locate the place of the exam – You have been sent a notice telling you when and where to report for the examination. If the location is in a different town or otherwise unfamiliar to you, it would be well to inquire the best route and learn something about the building.
- Relax the night before the test – Allow your mind to rest. Do not study at all that night. Plan some mild recreation or diversion; then go to bed early and get a good night's sleep.
- Get up early enough to make a leisurely trip to the place for the test – This way unforeseen events, traffic snarls, unfamiliar buildings, etc. will not upset you.
- Dress comfortably – A written test is not a fashion show. You will be known by number and not by name, so wear something comfortable.
- Leave excess paraphernalia at home – Shopping bags and odd bundles will get in your way. You need bring only the items mentioned in the official notice you received; usually everything you need is provided. Do not bring reference books to the exam. They will only confuse those last minutes and be taken away from you when in the test room.

- Arrive somewhat ahead of time – If because of transportation schedules you must get there very early, bring a newspaper or magazine to take your mind off yourself while waiting.
- Locate the examination room – When you have found the proper room, you will be directed to the seat or part of the room where you will sit. Sometimes you are given a sheet of instructions to read while you are waiting. Do not fill out any forms until you are told to do so; just read them and be prepared.
- Relax and prepare to listen to the instructions
- If you have any physical problem that may keep you from doing your best, be sure to tell the test administrator. If you are sick or in poor health, you really cannot do your best on the exam. You can come back and take the test some other time.

VII. AT THE TEST

The day of the test is here and you have the test booklet in your hand. The temptation to get going is very strong. Caution! There is more to success than knowing the right answers. You must know how to identify your papers and understand variations in the type of short-answer question used in this particular examination. Follow these suggestions for maximum results from your efforts:

1) Cooperate with the monitor

The test administrator has a duty to create a situation in which you can be as much at ease as possible. He will give instructions, tell you when to begin, check to see that you are marking your answer sheet correctly, and so on. He is not there to guard you, although he will see that your competitors do not take unfair advantage. He wants to help you do your best.

2) Listen to all instructions

Don't jump the gun! Wait until you understand all directions. In most civil service tests you get more time than you need to answer the questions. So don't be in a hurry. Read each word of instructions until you clearly understand the meaning. Study the examples, listen to all announcements and follow directions. Ask questions if you do not understand what to do.

3) Identify your papers

Civil service exams are usually identified by number only. You will be assigned a number; you must not put your name on your test papers. Be sure to copy your number correctly. Since more than one exam may be given, copy your exact examination title.

4) Plan your time

Unless you are told that a test is a "speed" or "rate of work" test, speed itself is usually not important. Time enough to answer all the questions will be provided, but this does not mean that you have all day. An overall time limit has been set. Divide the total time (in minutes) by the number of questions to determine the approximate time you have for each question.

5) Do not linger over difficult questions

If you come across a difficult question, mark it with a paper clip (useful to have along) and come back to it when you have been through the booklet. One caution if you do this – be sure to skip a number on your answer sheet as well. Check often to be sure that you have not lost your place and that you are marking in the row numbered the same as the question you are answering.

6) Read the questions

Be sure you know what the question asks! Many capable people are unsuccessful because they failed to read the questions correctly.

7) Answer all questions

Unless you have been instructed that a penalty will be deducted for incorrect answers, it is better to guess than to omit a question.

8) Speed tests

It is often better NOT to guess on speed tests. It has been found that on timed tests people are tempted to spend the last few seconds before time is called in marking answers at random – without even reading them – in the hope of picking up a few extra points. To discourage this practice, the instructions may warn you that your score will be "corrected" for guessing. That is, a penalty will be applied. The incorrect answers will be deducted from the correct ones, or some other penalty formula will be used.

9) Review your answers

If you finish before time is called, go back to the questions you guessed or omitted to give them further thought. Review other answers if you have time.

10) Return your test materials

If you are ready to leave before others have finished or time is called, take ALL your materials to the monitor and leave quietly. Never take any test material with you. The monitor can discover whose papers are not complete, and taking a test booklet may be grounds for disqualification.

VIII. EXAMINATION TECHNIQUES

1) Read the general instructions carefully. These are usually printed on the first page of the exam booklet. As a rule, these instructions refer to the timing of the examination; the fact that you should not start work until the signal and must stop work at a signal, etc. If there are any special instructions, such as a choice of questions to be answered, make sure that you note this instruction carefully.

2) When you are ready to start work on the examination, that is as soon as the signal has been given, read the instructions to each question booklet, underline any key words or phrases, such as least, best, outline, describe and the like. In this way you will tend to answer as requested rather than discover on reviewing your paper that you listed without describing, that you selected the worst choice rather than the best choice, etc.

3) If the examination is of the objective or multiple-choice type – that is, each question will also give a series of possible answers: A, B, C or D, and you are called upon to select the best answer and write the letter next to that answer on your answer paper – it is advisable to start answering each question in turn. There may be anywhere from 50 to 100 such questions in the three or four hours allotted and you can see how much time would be taken if you read through all the questions before beginning to answer any. Furthermore, if you

come across a question or group of questions which you know would be difficult to answer, it would undoubtedly affect your handling of all the other questions.

4) If the examination is of the essay type and contains but a few questions, it is a moot point as to whether you should read all the questions before starting to answer any one. Of course, if you are given a choice – say five out of seven and the like – then it is essential to read all the questions so you can eliminate the two that are most difficult. If, however, you are asked to answer all the questions, there may be danger in trying to answer the easiest one first because you may find that you will spend too much time on it. The best technique is to answer the first question, then proceed to the second, etc.

5) Time your answers. Before the exam begins, write down the time it started, then add the time allowed for the examination and write down the time it must be completed, then divide the time available somewhat as follows:
   - If 3-1/2 hours are allowed, that would be 210 minutes. If you have 80 objective-type questions, that would be an average of 2-1/2 minutes per question. Allow yourself no more than 2 minutes per question, or a total of 160 minutes, which will permit about 50 minutes to review.
   - If for the time allotment of 210 minutes there are 7 essay questions to answer, that would average about 30 minutes a question. Give yourself only 25 minutes per question so that you have about 35 minutes to review.

6) The most important instruction is to read each question and make sure you know what is wanted. The second most important instruction is to time yourself properly so that you answer every question. The third most important instruction is to answer every question. Guess if you have to but include something for each question. Remember that you will receive no credit for a blank and will probably receive some credit if you write something in answer to an essay question. If you guess a letter – say "B" for a multiple-choice question – you may have guessed right. If you leave a blank as an answer to a multiple-choice question, the examiners may respect your feelings but it will not add a point to your score. Some exams may penalize you for wrong answers, so in such cases only, you may not want to guess unless you have some basis for your answer.

7) Suggestions
   a. Objective-type questions
      1. Examine the question booklet for proper sequence of pages and questions
      2. Read all instructions carefully
      3. Skip any question which seems too difficult; return to it after all other questions have been answered
      4. Apportion your time properly; do not spend too much time on any single question or group of questions
      5. Note and underline key words – all, most, fewest, least, best, worst, same, opposite, etc.
      6. Pay particular attention to negatives
      7. Note unusual option, e.g., unduly long, short, complex, different or similar in content to the body of the question
      8. Observe the use of "hedging" words – probably, may, most likely, etc.

9. Make sure that your answer is put next to the same number as the question
10. Do not second-guess unless you have good reason to believe the second answer is definitely more correct
11. Cross out original answer if you decide another answer is more accurate; do not erase until you are ready to hand your paper in
12. Answer all questions; guess unless instructed otherwise
13. Leave time for review

b. Essay questions
1. Read each question carefully
2. Determine exactly what is wanted. Underline key words or phrases.
3. Decide on outline or paragraph answer
4. Include many different points and elements unless asked to develop any one or two points or elements
5. Show impartiality by giving pros and cons unless directed to select one side only
6. Make and write down any assumptions you find necessary to answer the questions
7. Watch your English, grammar, punctuation and choice of words
8. Time your answers; don't crowd material

8) Answering the essay question

Most essay questions can be answered by framing the specific response around several key words or ideas. Here are a few such key words or ideas:

M's: manpower, materials, methods, money, management
P's: purpose, program, policy, plan, procedure, practice, problems, pitfalls, personnel, public relations

a. Six basic steps in handling problems:
1. Preliminary plan and background development
2. Collect information, data and facts
3. Analyze and interpret information, data and facts
4. Analyze and develop solutions as well as make recommendations
5. Prepare report and sell recommendations
6. Install recommendations and follow up effectiveness

b. Pitfalls to avoid
1. Taking things for granted – A statement of the situation does not necessarily imply that each of the elements is necessarily true; for example, a complaint may be invalid and biased so that all that can be taken for granted is that a complaint has been registered
2. Considering only one side of a situation – Wherever possible, indicate several alternatives and then point out the reasons you selected the best one
3. Failing to indicate follow up – Whenever your answer indicates action on your part, make certain that you will take proper follow-up action to see how successful your recommendations, procedures or actions turn out to be
4. Taking too long in answering any single question – Remember to time your answers properly

EXAMINATION SECTION

EXAMINATION SECTION

TEST 1

DIRECTIONS: Each question or incomplete statement is followed by several suggested answers or completions. Select the one that BEST answers the question or completes the statement. *PRINT THE LETTER OF THE CORRECT ANSWER IN THE SPACE AT THE RIGHT.*

1. In their studies of the heavens, the Babylonians tried to
   A. predict the occurrence of "guest stars"
   B. make geometrical models of the motions of celestial objects
   C. predict the future positions of celestial objects
   D. make geometrical models of celestial objects

   1.____

2. The period of the Earth's revolution about the Sun is
   A. 365¼ days   B. none of these
   C. 364¼ days   D. 366¼ days

   2.____

3. A possible synodic period of a superior planet is
   A. 365¼ days   B. none of these
   C. 364¼ days   D. 366¼ days

   3.____

4. During the year, the Sun appears to move with respect to the stars along
   A. the ecliptic   B. the celestial equator
   C. the horizon   D. a deferent

   4.____

5. For which of the following did the model of Eudeoxus NOT account?
   A. Retrograde motion
   B. Changes in brightness of the planets
   C. Inclination of planetary orbits
   D. Diurnal motion

   5.____

6. The model of Eudoxus consisted of
   A. epicycles and deferents
   B. eccentrics
   C. elliptical motions
   D. concentric spheres with various points of attachment

   6.____

7. An essential assumption made by Eratosthenes when he measured the size of the Earth was that
   A. the Sun was nearby
   B. the Earth could be considered flat if one was concerned only with small areas
   C. the Earth was spherical
   D. Alexandria was generally north of Syene

   7.____

8. The obtaining of a reasonable result for the ratio of the Earth-Sun distance to the Earth-Moon distance by Aristarchus must be considered fortuitous because
   A. the Sun is further away than he thought
   B. the Moon's orbit is not circular
   C. the Moon's motion is not uniform
   D. all of the above

9. Ptolemy's model of the universe was based upon the assumption that
   A. uniform motion in a straight line is the most natural motion for a celestial object
   B. the Earth is at the center of the orbits of the planets
   C. uniform motion in a circle is the most natural motion for a celestial object
   D. celestial objects are pulled into circular orbits by gravity

10. The Sun moves with respect to the stars about _____ per day.
    A. 24°   B. 0°   C. ½°   D. 1°

11. To locate an object in space one needs _____ coordinate(s).
    A. one   B. two   C. three   D. four

12. To locate an object on the celestial sphere, one needs _____ coordinate(s).
    A. one   B. two   C. three   D. four

Questions 13-16.

DIRECTIONS: Match the letter of the CORRECT choice with Questions 13 through 16.

   A. Eastward along the celestial equator from the Vernal Equinox
   B. Along the horizon from the north point through the east point
   C. Along a vertical circle from the horizon
   D. Along an hour circle from the celestial equator

13. Right ascension is measured.

14. Declination is measured.

15. Altitude is measured.

16. Azimuth is measured.

Questions 17-18.

DIRECTIONS: Questions 17 and 18 are to be answered on the basis of the following diagram.

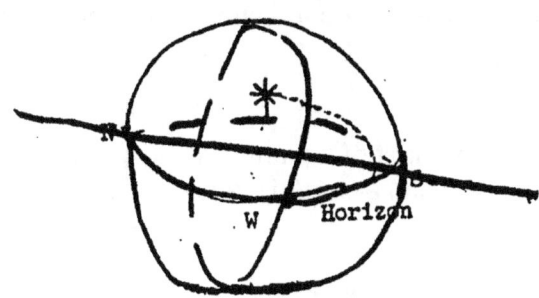

17. In the diagram shown at the right of a part of the celestial sphere, what is the altitude of the star? The star is west of the meridian and the observer's latitude is 0°.
    A. 90°   B. 45°   C. 270°   D. 0°

17.____

18. What is the declination of the star?
    A. 90°   B. 45°   C. 270°   D. 0°

18.____

19. What is the sidereal period of an inferior planet whose synodic period is ¾ year?
    A. - 3 year   B. -$^1/_3$ year   C. $^7/_3$ year   D. $^3/_7$ year

19.____

20. What is the synodic period of a superior planet whose sidereal period is 5 years?
    A. -$^5/_4$ year   B. $^5/_4$ year   C. $^4/_5$ year   D. $^5/_6$ year

20.____

21. The synodic period of a planet is the time it takes to
    A. revolve about the Sun
    B. revolve about the Earth
    C. move around the sky with respect to the stars
    D. move around the sky with respect to the Sun

21.____

22. The Copernican Theory
    A. did away with the equant
    B. put the Sun at the center of the orbits of the planets
    C. put the earth at the center of the orbits of the planets
    D. did away with epicycles

22.____

23. The MAIN contribution of Tycho to astronomy was
    A. accurate observations of the positions of the planets
    B. the discovery of a new star
    C. an improved model of the solar system
    D. the study of motion of a great comet

23.____

24. To determine the distance of an inferior planet from the Sun in astronomical units, one needs to know
    A. the sidereal period
    B. the angle between the planet and the sun at the greatest elongation
    C. either A or B
    D. both A and B

25. What is the eccentricity of the orbit of a planet whose MAXIMUM and MINIMUM distances from the sun are 1 A.U. and ¼ A.U.?
    A. $3/5$ B. $5/4$ C. $2/5$ D. $5/8$

KEY (CORRECT ANSWERS)

1.	C	11.	C
2.	A	12.	B
3.	D	13.	A
4.	A	14.	D
5.	B	15.	C
6.	D	16.	B
7.	C	17.	B
8.	D	18.	D
9.	C	19.	D
10.	D	20.	B

21. D
22. B
23. A
24. C
25. A

TEST 2

DIRECTIONS: Each question or incomplete statement is followed by several suggested answers or completions. Select the one that BEST answers the question or completes the statement. *PRINT THE LETTER OF THE CORRECT ANSWER IN THE SPACE AT THE RIGHT.*

1. What is the MINIMUM distance from the sun of a planet whose orbit has an eccentricity of ½ and a semimajor axis of 2 A.U.?   1.____
   A. 1 A.U. B. 2 A.U.
   C. 3 A.U. D. None of the above

2. What would be the period of this planet?   2.____
   A. 1 year   B. $\sqrt[3]{4}$ years   C. 8 years   D. $\sqrt{8}$ years

3. What is the gravitational attraction between two people when: 3.____
   $m_1 = 100 \times 10^3$ gm $m_2 = 60 \times 10^3$ gm
   dist = 20 cm $G = 7 \times 10^{-8}$ dynes cm^2 gm^{-2}
   Consider that they act as point masses.
   A. $\frac{42}{2} \times 10^0$ dynes   B. $\frac{42}{2} \times 10^{-1}$ dynes
   C. $\frac{42}{2} \times 10^3$ dynes   D. $\frac{42}{2} \times 10^{19}$ dynes

4. How much would a 100-pound person weigh on Jupiter? The mass of Jupiter is about 300 times that of the Earth, and its radius is about 11 times that of the Earth.   4.____
   A. $100 \times \frac{300}{(11)}$ lb.   B. $100 \times \frac{300}{(11)^2}$ lb.
   C. $100 \times \frac{7 \times 10^{-8} \times 300}{(11)^2}$ lb.   D. $100 \times \frac{7 \times 10^{-8} \times 300 \times 100}{(11)^2}$ lb.

5. What would be the acceleration of gravity on Mars? The mass of Mars is about $^1/_{10}$ that of the Earth, and the radius of Mars is about ½ that of the Earth.   5.____
   A. 2/5   B. 1/5
   C. 50   D. None of the above

6. A parabolic orbit is one in which the object   6.____
   A. has a velocity equal to $\sqrt{2}$ times the circular velocity
   B. will escape from the object about which it is orbiting
   C. both A and B
   D. neither A nor B

5

7. How long will it take a space probe to go from the Earth to Jupiter on a minimum energy transfer orbit? The semimajor axis of Jupiter's orbit is about 5 A.U., and of the Earth's orbit is 1 A.U.

   A. ½ ($4^{3/2}$)   B. $3^{3/2}$ C. ½ ($3^{3/2}$)   D. ½ ($6^{3/2}$)

7.____

8. A proof that the Earth rotates is the
   A. diurnal motion
   B. change of directions of a Foucault pendulum
   C. wind
   D. seasons

8.____

9. The mass of the Earth can be measured by
   A. comparing the attraction between the Earth and a given mass, M_A, to the attraction between another mass, M_B and M_A
   B. multiplying the density of a small sample of the Earth by the volume of the Earth
   C. measuring the altitude of stars from different, known positions on the Earth
   D. none of the abaove

9.____

10. The presently accepted age of the Earth is about _____ years
    A. 10 million   B. 1 billion   C. 4 billion   D. 10 billion

10.____

11. At the North Pole, the stars appear to move in circles around
    A. the north point on the horizon
    B. a point 45° between the north point on the horizon and the zenith
    C. the zenith
    D. the south point on the horizon

11.____

12. The speed at the Equator due to the Earth's rotation is about _____ miles/hour.
    A. 1,000   B. 750   C. 0   D. 500

12.____

13. About what time of day or night does the Moon rise when it is full?
    A. Midnight   B. Sunrise   C. Noon   D. Sunset

13.____

14. Which of the following can NEVER appear at opposition?
    A. Saturn   B. Moon   C. Mars   D. Sun

14.____

15. Suppose you were an astronaut in orbit about the Earth and you wish to catch up with another spacecraft in the same orbit as you but some distance ahead. You should
    A. fire rockets to increase your speed
    B. fire rockets to decrease your speed
    C. radio for help
    D. give up

15.____

16. It is December, and the Moon is in its new phase. An observer on Earth is   16.____
    A. in the umbra of the Moon's shadow
    B. in the penumbra of the Moon's shadow
    C. not in the Moon's shadow, but in the Earth's shadow
    D. not in either the Moon's or the Earth's shadow

17. It is December, and Mars and Jupiter are simultaneously at opposition.   17.____
    A. Neither planet shows retrograde motion.
    B. Both planets show retrograde motion.
    C. Only one planet can show retrograde motion.
    D. Insufficient information to determine whether retrograde motion occurs.

18. The sidereal period of Venus is 0.615 years. How long is the period between   18.____
    two successive superior conjunctions of Venus?
    A. 0.615 years   B. 1.000 years   C. 1.598 years   D. 2.628 years

19. Pluto's distance from the Sun varies from 30 A.U. to 50 A.U. What is the   19.____
    APPROXIMATE eccentricity of its orbit?
    A. .250   B. .400   C. .600   D. .666

20. A satellite in orbit is hit by a meteor of a thousandth its mass but equal   20.____
    momentum coming from the opposite direction. The meteor remains imbedded
    in the vehicle. The satellite
    A. slows slightly   B. is thrown out into space
    C. goes into a lower orbit   D. drops straight down

21. An astronaut in orbit is taking a "space walk" outside of his spacecraft.   21.____
    He leaves a tool floating in space several hundred feet in front of the spacecraft
    (ahead of it in the same orbit with the same orbital velocity).
    A. It remains at this same relative position in the spacecraft's orbit.
    B. It orbits the spacecraft at a distance of about several hundred feet from it.
    C. It slowly moves toward the spacecraft.
    D. It slowly moves away from the spacecraft.

22. Two stars, each having a mass equal to that of the Sun, revolve about   22.____
    their barycenter at 1.0 A.U. from it. Their period of revolution is _____ sidereal
    years.
    A. 0.5   B. 1.0   C. 2.0   D. 4.0

23. Which of the following orbital parameters from the solar system is defined   23.____
    with respect to the Earth's orbit?
    A. Period   B. Eccentricity
    C. Perihelion   D. Inclination

24. Which of Newton's laws governs the path of an object in orbit about the Sun?   24.____
    A. First Law, momentum conserved
    B. Second Law, force = mass × acceleration
    C. Third Law, forces are mutual
    D. All of the above

25. Eclipses of the Sun can occur when the Earth is APPROXIMATELY at   25._____
    A. perihelion   B. the line of nodes
    C. aphelion   D. any point in the Earth's orbit

KEY (CORRECT ANSWERS)

1. A
2. D
3. B
4. B
5. A

6. C
7. C
8. B
9. A
10. C

11. C
12. A
13. D
14. D
15. A

16. D
17. B
18. C
19. C
20. D

21. C
22. C
23. D
24. D
25. B

TEST 3

DIRECTIONS: Each question or incomplete statement is followed by several suggested answers or completions. Select the one that BEST answers the question or completes the statement. *PRINT THE LETTER OF THE CORRECT ANSWER IN THE SPACE AT THE RIGHT.*

1. The longitude 51° can also be expressed as
   A. 51^h B. 12^h12^m C. $3^h1\text{-}\tfrac{1}{2}^m$ D. 3^h24^m

   1.____

2. The non-uniformity of apparent solar time is caused by
   A. eccentricity of the Earth's orbit
   B. the inclination of the ecliptic to the celestial equator
   C. both A and B
   D. neither A nor B

   2.____

3. The rotation of the Earth provides a uniform measure of the passage of time.
   A. True B. False
   C. Relative D. Impossible to determine

   3.____

4. The Gregorian calendar differs from the Julian calendar by
   A. omitting the 13th month in "full years"
   B. giving even-numbered months 30 days and odd-numbered months 31 days
   C. omitting three leap years in every 400 years
   D. having century years divisible by 400 not be leap years

   4.____

5. On November 7, sidereal time is about _____ solar time.
   A. 3 hours behind B. 3 hours ahead of
   C. 15 hours behind D. 15 hours ahead of

   5.____

6. In the first part of November, an accurate sundial in Philadelphia (longitude 75°W reads 12 Noon. What is the Central Standard Time?
   A. 11:43 A.M. B. 12:17 P.M. C. 10:43 A.M. D. 11:17 A.M.

   6.____

7. What is the longitude if the local mean solar time is 16^h23^m and UT is 5^h00^m?
   A. 11^h23^m East B. 11^h23^m West
   C. 21^h23^m East D. 21^h23^m West

   7.____

8. What is the local hour angle of a star whose right ascension is 2^h30^m if the local sidereal time is 30^m?
   A. 2^h East B. 2^h West C. 3^h East D. 3^h West

   8.____

9. X-rays have a wavelength that is _____ visible light.
   A. longer than
   B. shorter than
   C. equal to
   D. sometimes longer and sometimes shorter than

   9.____

10. What is the wavelength of radio waves whose frequency is 100 kilocycles, i.e., 10^5 c/s? The speed of light is 3×10^{10} cm/sec.
    A. $1/3 \times 10^{-5}$ cm
    B. 3×10^2 cm
    C. 3×10^5 cm
    D. 3×10^{15} cm

11. What will be the angle that reflected sunlight will make with the surface of a pond if the altitude of the Sun is 30°?
    A. 0°
    B. 30°
    C. 60°
    D. 90°

12. If the arrows represent the path of a ray of light, then medium A has a _____ index of refraction than medium B.
    A. higher
    B. lower
    C. equal
    D. one cannot tell from the information given

13. One loses half of the image if one covers up half of the objective lens of a telescope.
    A. True
    B. False
    C. Sometimes true
    D. One cannot tell from the information given

Questions 14-16.

DIRECTIONS: In answering Questions 14 through 16, consider the images produced by two telescopes.

	A	B
Aperture	10 in.	5 in.
Focal Length	120 in.	40 in.

14. The scale of the images produced by A would be _____ that of B.
    A. 1/3
    B. ½
    C. 2 times
    D. 3 times

15. The image of Mars would be _____ as bright in A as in B.
    A. 4/9
    B. 9/4
    C. 4 times
    D. 9 times

16. The image of a star would be _____ as bright in A as in B.
    A. 4/9
    B. 9/4
    C. 4 times
    D. 9 times

3 (#3)

17. What magnification would be required to resolve an object 1.2 miles across on the Moon with a one-inch telescope on the Earth. (The distance of the Moon is 140,000 mi.; there are approximately 2×10^5 sec of arc in 1 rad.; and assume the unaided eye can resolve objects 1' across).
    A. 15X
    B. 60X
    C. 2.4×10^{12}X
    D. Cannot be done no matter how high the magnification

17.____

18. Which of the following does one usually NOT have in an equatorial telescope mounting?
    A. One axis pointing to the celestial pole
    B. One axis pointing to the zenith
    C. Two mutually perpendicular axes
    D. A clock drive

18.____

19. Which type of telescope would be BEST for photographing the spectra of faint stars with a large spectrograph?
    A. Refractor   B. Reflector   C. Schmidt   D. Electron

19.____

20. What focal length eyepiece should be used to get 100X magnification with a telescope which has a 5-inch diameter objective with a 50-inch focal length?
    A. $\frac{1}{20}$ in.   B. ½ in.   C. 2 in.   D. 20 in.

20.____

21. Which of the following is NOT usually part of a spectrograph?
    A. Slit   B. Camera lens
    C. Eyepiece   D. Collimating lens

21.____

22. If a star is coming towards us, its spectrum is shifted to
    A. shorter wavelengths   B. longer wavelengths
    C. ultraviolet   D. infrared

22.____

23. The reason one cannot photograph extremely fine detail on the Moon with the largest telescope is:
    A. Poor optical quality of the telescopes
    B. Insufficient magnification
    C. Turbulence in the Earth's atmosphere
    D. Graininess of photographic plates

23.____

24. Albedo is
    A. the amount of light incident on a body
    B. the fraction of the incident light reflected by a body
    C. the fraction of the incident light absorbed by a body
    D. a measure of the color of a body

24.____

25. The Moon moves _____ °/day with respect to the stars as seen from the Earth.   25._____

A. $\dfrac{29\frac{1}{2}}{360}$ B. $\dfrac{27\frac{1}{3}}{360}$ C. $\dfrac{360}{29\frac{1}{2}}$ D. $\dfrac{360}{27\frac{1}{3}}$

KEY (CORRECT ANSWERS)

1. D
2. C
3. B
4. C
5. B

6. C
7. A
8. B
9. B
10. C

11. B
12. A
13. B
14. D
15. A

16. C
17. D
18. B
19. B
20. A

21. C
22. A
23. C
24. B
25. D

TEST 4

DIRECTIONS: Each question or incomplete statement is followed by several suggested answers or completions. Select the one that BEST answers the question or completes the statement. *PRINT THE LETTER OF THE CORRECT ANSWER IN THE SPACE AT THE RIGHT.*

1. What is the phase of the Moon if it is on the meridian at 6 P.M.?
   A. New   B. 1st quarter   C. Full   D. 3rd quarter

   1.____

2. If M is the mass of the Moon, R its radius, and D its distance from the Earth, the surface gravity, g, of the moon is given by g =

   A. $\dfrac{M}{\frac{4}{3}\pi R^3}$ B. $\dfrac{GM}{R}$ C. $\dfrac{GM}{D^2}$ D. $\dfrac{GM}{R^2}$

   2.____

3. The evidence that the Moon does not have an extensive atmosphere consists of all of the following EXCEPT:
   A. Occasional mists on floors of some craters
   B. Thermal velocity of molecules not much less than the escape velocity
   C. No gradual dimming of stars as they are occulted by the Moon
   D. Well-defined shadows

   3.____

4. Suppose a mountain is observed on the Moon 100 miles from the terminator. Its shadow is 20 miles long. The diameter of the Moon is 2,000 miles. How high is the mountain?
   A. ½ mile   B. 1 mile   C. 2 miles   D. 5 miles

   4.____

5. The motion of the nodes of the Moon's orbit is _____ along the ecliptic.
   A. eastward   B. westward   C. northward   D. southward

   5.____

6. Eclipses of the Sun may NOT be used to
   A. study the thermal properties of the Moon
   B. determine the relative locations of the Sun, Moon, and Earth
   C. study the corona of the Sun
   D. study the chromosphere of the Sun

   6.____

7.

   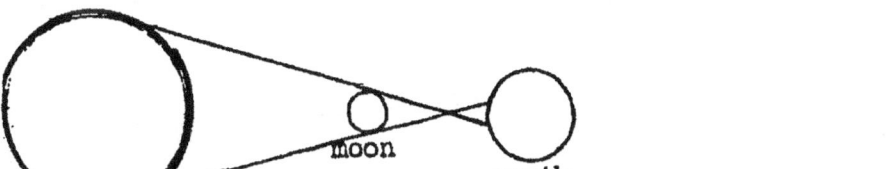

   The eclipse shown above is a(n)
   A. annular eclipse of the Sun   B. partial eclipse of the Sun
   C. total eclipse of the Sun   D. partial eclipse of the Moon

   7.____

13

8. An eclipse of the Sun can occur only when
   A. the Sun is above the horizon
   B. the Sun is near the line of nodes of the Moon's orbit
   C. the Moon is full
   D. there are no clouds

9. If the semi-major axis of the Earth's orbit were 5 A.U., but the Moon remained at its present distance from the Earth, what would the frequency of total eclipses of the Sun be?
   A. More frequent
   B. Less frequent
   C. Unchanged
   D. One cannot determine from the information given

10. The evidence that tides are caused by the Moon and the Sun is:
    A. High tide occurs when the Moon is on the meridian
    B. Exactly two high tides occur between successive times when the Moon is on the meridian
    C. The smallest tides occur when the moon is at first and third quarters
    D. Choices B and C

11. Tides are produced by
    A. the Moon's pulling the water away from the Earth
    B. a magnetic attraction of the Moon for the water
    C. the component of the tidal force perpendicular to the Earth's surface
    D. the component of the tidal force parallel to the Earth's surface

12. An example of a differential gravitational force is
    A. the difference in force of attraction on one object by two other objects
    B. the difference in force of attraction on two objects by a third object
    C. a vector
    D. the difference between gravitational force and proximity

13. The precession of the Earth is caused by
    A. the attraction of the Sun and Moon for the equatorial bulge of the Earth
    B. the attraction of the other planets for the Earth
    C. the rotation of the Earth
    D. all of the above

14. The period of precession of the Earth is about _____ year(s).
    A. 1   B. 50   C. 360   D. 26,000

15. Which satellite would have the GREATER period, one a million miles from the center of the Earth or one a million miles from the center of Jupiter?
    A. Earth
    B. Jupiter
    C. Both would be equal
    D. One cannot determine from the information given

16. The barycenter of two bodies is
    A. the center of one of the bodies
    B. the center of mass (or gravity) of the two
    C. a point halfway between the two
    D. the line joining the two

17. The location of the Trojan Asteroids at two points along Jupiter's orbit is a
    A. special case of perturbation theory
    B. coincidence of orbital distance from the Sun, but they could be anywhere along Jupiter's orbit
    C. special case of the n-body problem
    D. coincidence of orbital distance from Jupiter, but unrelated to their distance from the Sun

18. At what points on the Earth would objects fall straight toward the center of the planet when dropped from a high tower on the surface?
    A. At all points
    B. At the equator only
    C. At the poles only
    D. At the equator and the poles

19. The tidal bulges are caused by
    A. the differential gravitational forces of the Sun and the Moon
    B. the motions of the Sun, Earth, and Moon producing a centrifugal effect
    C. both A and B together
    D. both A and B in combination with the rotation of the Earth

20. The solid surface of the Earth is NOT deformed by
    A. the rotation of the Earth
    B. tidal effects due to the Moon and the Sun
    C. the weight of the continental masses
    D. the precession of the Earth

21. The altitude-azimuth coordinate system would be used for
    A. monitoring the ascent of a weather balloon
    B. observing a satellite trajectory
    C. determining the relative position of two stars
    D. determining the absolute position of a star

22. The Earth's rotation period with respect to the stars
    A. was exactly 24 hours in 1900
    B. is different at aphelion and perihelion
    C. is increasing at 1/1000 second per century
    D. is decreased slightly by the precession of the equinoxes

23. The Earth's period of revolution about the Sun with respect to the stars is
    A. about 365¼ solar days
    B. the basis of our calendar
    C. decreasing at 1/1000 second per century
    D. decreased slightly by the precession of the equinoxes

24. In measuring the distance to the Moon by laser or by radar, we measure the _____ the transmitted and reflected pulses.
    A. speed of
    B. intensity of
    C. time between
    D. wavelength of

    24.____

25. In which of the following is there no first, second, third, or last contact?
    A. Total eclipse
    B. Partial eclipse
    C. Annular eclipse
    D. Penumbral eclipse

    25.____

KEY (CORRECT ANSWERS)

1.	B	11.	D
2.	D	12.	B
3.	A	13.	D
4.	C	14.	D
5.	B	15.	B
6.	A	16.	B
7.	A	17.	C
8.	B	18.	C
9.	A	19.	C
10.	D	20.	D

21. A
22. C
23. A
24. C
25. D

TEST 5

DIRECTIONS: Each question or incomplete statement is followed by several suggested answers or completions. Select the one that BEST answers the question or completes the statement. *PRINT THE LETTER OF THE CORRECT ANSWER IN THE SPACE AT THE RIGHT.*

1. In order to predict when the moon will first be visible after it is new, one must know all of the following EXCEPT the
   A. apparent angular speeds of the Sun and the Moon
   B. relative distances of the Sun and the Moon
   C. angle between the ecliptic and the horizon
   D. angular distance of the Moon from the ecliptic

   1.____

2. The time interval from full moon to full moon is called the _____ period of the Moon.
   A. sidereal   B. synodic   C. waxing   D. temporal

   2.____

3. The full moon sets at sunrise.
   A. True
   B. False
   C. Sometimes
   D. Relative to the time of the month

   3.____

4. Suppose you observed that a particular star was 20° above the horizon when it was on the meridian. After taking 10^6 steps due north, you observed that this star was only $10°$ above the horizon when it was on the meridian. What is the circumference of the planet you are on? (Assume the planet is spherical.)
   A. 18×10^6 steps
   B. 36×10^6 steps
   C. 360×10^6 steps
   D. 7200×10^6 steps

   4.____

5. In order to determine the relative sizes of the Sun, Moon, and the Earth, as was done by Aristarchus, one needs to know all of the following EXCEPT:
   A. The relative distances of the Sun and the Moon from the Earth
   B. The angular sizes of the Sun and the Moon as seen from the Earth
   C. The size of the Earth's shadow at the distance of the Moon, relative to the diameter of the Moon
   D. The distance of the Moon from the Earth

   5.____

6. The Greeks had to adopt models for the motions of the planets that were more complex than uniform motion in circles centered on the Earth because this simple model
   A. conflicted with their religious views
   B. did not explain the synodic periods of the planets
   C. did not explain retrograde motion
   D. none of the above

   6.____

7. Copernicus eliminated all but one of the following features of Ptolemy's model of the planetary system. Which did he NOT eliminate?
   A. The equant
   B. The centers of the epicycles of Mercury and Venus being on the Earth-Sun line
   C. The center of the epicycle-planet line being parallel to the Earth-Sun line for Mars, Jupiter, and Saturn
   D. Epicycles

   7.____

8. What is the sidereal period of an inferior planet whose synodic period is $2/3$ year?
   A. $2/5$ year   B. $3/5$ year   C. $5/3$ year   D. $5/2$ year

   8.____

9. Suppose the greatest elongation of a planet is observed to be 45°, then the planet is a(n) _____ planet.
   A. inferior   B. superior   C. intermodal   D. double

   9.____

10. What is the distance of the planet in the previous question from the Sun in AU?
    A. $\frac{1}{\sqrt{2}}$ B. 1   C. $\sqrt{2}$ D. 2

    10.____

11. The MAJOR contribution of Tycho Brahe to astronomy was
    A. the discovery of the nova in Cassiopeia in 1572
    B. the discovery of the great comet of 1577
    C. his observations of the positions of planets
    D. his model of the planetary system

    11.____

12. What is the eccentricity of the orbit of a planet whose perihelion distance is 1×10^9 miles and whose aphelion distance is 2×10^9 miles?
    A. 0   B. $1/3$ C. $½$ D. 3

    12.____

13. At aphelion, the speed of the planet in the previous question will be _____ its speed at perihelion.
    A. ½
    B. the same as
    C. 2 times
    D. none of the above

    13.____

14. What is the sidereal period of this planet? (One AU is about 10^8 miles.)
    A. $(15)^{2/3}$ year
    B. $(15)^{3/2}$ year
    C. $(15)^{1/2}$ year
    D. None of the above

    14.____

15. If you saw an object moving in a circle, you should conclude that
    A. a force is acting on the object
    B. the object wants to go in a circle
    C. angels are pushing the object
    D. it is in an equal magnetic field

    15.____

16. The mass of an object is determined by a spring balance.   16.____
    A. True
    B. False
    C. Possibly
    D. Cannot be determined from the information given

17. In the absence of friction, if you set an object moving on a level surface, it   17.____
    would eventually come to a stop.
    A. True
    B. False
    C. Possibly
    D. Cannot be determined from the information given

18. It is possible to drive around a banked curve in an icy road with sliding.   18.____
    A. True
    B. False
    C. Possibly
    D. Cannot be determined from the information given

19. Gravitationally, spheres act as point masses.   19.____
    A. True
    B. False
    C. Possibly
    D. Cannot be determined from the information given

20. Gravitation is the strongest force we know.   20.____
    A. True
    B. False
    C. Possibly
    D. Cannot be determined from the information given

21. If one doubles the distance between two masses, the gravitational force   21.____
    between them _____ by a factor of _____.
    A. decreases; four   B. decreases; two
    C. increases; two   D. increases; four

22. If one doubles the mass of one object while keeping the other mass and   22.____
    the distance between the two masses the same, the gravitational force on the
    first mass
    A. decreases by a factor of four   B. decreases by a factor of two
    C. is unchanged   D. increases by a factor of two

23. The acceleration experienced by an object in the gravitational field of   23.____
    the Earth depends on the mass of the object.
    A. True
    B. False
    C. Sometimes
    D. Cannot be determined from the information given

24. If the gravitational attraction experienced by one mass as a result of a second mass doubles, then the attraction experienced by the second mass due to the first also doubles.
    A. True
    B. False
    C. Sometimes
    D. Cannot be determined from the information given

25. Callisto is a satellite of the planet Jupiter. It is about 5 times as far from the center of Jupiter as the Moon is from the center of the Earth, and its orbital period is about 5/10 that of the Moon about the Earth. Using this data, what is the ratio of the mass of Jupiter to the mass of the Earth?
    A. 1/500   B. 1/200   C. 200   D. 500

KEY (CORRECT ANSWERS)

1. B		11. C	
2. B		12. B	
3. A		13. A	
4. B		14. B	
5. D		15. A	
6. C		16. B	
7. D		17. B	
8. A		18. A	
9. A		19. A	
10. A		20. B	

21. A
22. D
23. B
24. A
25. D

EXAMINATION SECTION
TEST 1

DIRECTIONS: Each question or incomplete statement is followed by several suggested answers or completions. Select the one that BEST answers the question or completes the statement. *PRINT THE LETTER OF THE CORRECT ANSWER IN THE SPACE AT THE RIGHT.*

1. If the speed of an object in a circular orbit around the Earth is V mi/hr, then its speed would have to increase to at least _____ in order to escape from the Earth.
   A. $\sqrt{2}$V mi/hr
   B. 2V mi/hr
   C. Neither of the above
   D. Not enough information

2. In order to determine the age of the Earth from the decay of uranium into lead, it is sufficient to know the decay rates of U^{235} and U^{238}, the present concentrations of the isotopes of uranium and lead in the rock sample, and to assume that the lead ore solidified when the Earth was formed.
   A. True
   B. False
   C. Possibly
   D. Cannot be determined from the information given

3. One of the pieces of evidence that the relative positions of the continents may not have been the same in the past as they are at present is the existence of "magnetic anomalies" on the ocean floor.
   A. True
   B. False
   C. Possibly
   D. Cannot be determined from the information given

4. The interior of the Earth is thought to be solid throughout.
   A. True
   B. False
   C. Possibly
   D. Cannot be determined from the information given

5. One of the proofs that the Earth rotates is
   A. diurnal motion
   B. the phases of the moon
   C. the aberration of starlight
   D. the behavior of a Foucault pendulum

6. The star Capella (Dec. +46°) is circumpolar from Ann Arbor, Michigan (Lat. +32°).
   A. True
   B. False
   C. Possibly
   D. Cannot be determined from the information given

   6.____

7. The bright star Antares (Dec. -26°) appears to pass overheat at Tucson, Arizona (Lat. +32°).
   A. True
   B. False
   C. Possibly
   D. Cannot be determined from the information given

   7.____

8. One of the proofs that the Earth revolves about the Sun is
   A. diurnal motion
   B. the annual motion of the Sun
   C. the aberration of starlight
   D. the behavior of a Foucault pendulum

   8.____

9. A superior planet has a sidereal period that is _____ an inferior planet.
   A. greater than   B. less than
   C. equal to   D. indefinite when compared to

   9.____

10. The MAJOR cause of the seasons is the ellipticity of the Earth's orbit.
    A. True
    B. False
    C. Possibly
    D. Cannot be determined from the information given

    10.____

11. Aurora, "Northern Lights," are caused by
    A. thunderstorms
    B. sunlight reflected from the polar icecap
    C. charged particles hitting the Earth's atmosphere
    D. vivid imaginations

    11.____

12. What is the MINIMUM distance from the sun of a planet whose orbit has an eccentricity of ¼ and a semimajor axis of 4 A.U.?
    A. 1 A.U.   B. 2 A.U.   C. 3 A.U.   D. 4 A.U.

    12.____

13. As seen from the Earth, the Moon appears to move about _____ with respect to the stars.
    A. 1° per day   B. 13° per day
    C. 24° per day   D. None of the above

    13.____

14. Declination is measured
    A. eastward along the celestial equator from the Vernal Equinox
    B. along the horizon from the north point through the east point
    C. along a vertical circle from the horizon
    D. along an hour circle from the celestial equator

14.____

15. The presently accepted age of the Earth is about _____ years.
    A. 5 million   B. 1 billion   C. 5 billion   D. 10 billion

15.____

16. The material in comets is probably MOST like
    A. the interstellar medium   B. the interplanetary medium
    C. present day planetary material   D. primeval solar system material

16.____

17. The material in asteroids is probably MOST like
    A. the interstellar medium   B. the interplanetary medium
    C. present day planetary material   D. primeval solar system material

17.____

18. The following characteristic of the solar system is MAINLY due to the heating effect of the primeval sun.
    A. The planets are separated by increasingly large gaps at increasing distance from the Sun.
    B. Planetary masses are greatest at an intermediate distance from the Sun.
    C. The planets revolve about the Sun in the same direction.
    D. The planets tend to be in nearly circular orbits.

18.____

19. Jupiter seems to be radiating more heat than it receives from the Sun, and appears less frigid than it should be. Without an inner heat source, its temperature depends on the amount of solar radiation
    A. that strikes it   B. it reflects
    C. it absorbs   D. it emits

19.____

20. Pluto's orbit is more eccentric and has a higher inclination than any other planet. From this we can deduce that Pluto
    A. is not an original member of the solar system
    B. must have been strongly deflected at some time in order to throw it out of its original circular orbit
    C. has not been sufficiently perturbed to bring it into a circular orbit in the ecliptic plane
    D. must be a kind of comet

20.____

21. Mars has retained much less atmosphere than the Earth because its escape velocity is _____ than the molecular speed for most gases, but Earth's is _____.
    A. less; greater   B. greater; less
    C. less; much less   D. greater; much greater

21.____

22. The inside of Saturn's rings rotates faster than the outside. This occurs because
    A. orbital velocity decreases with increasing distance from the center of mass
    B. perturbations are produced by Saturn's moons
    C. the equatorial bulge of Saturn produces an additional component of force
    D. the atmosphere of Saturn, rotating rapidly with the planet, "drags" the inner part along with it

22.____

23. If the spectrum of a planet shows dark lines which are not present in the solar spectrum,
    A. some gas is present in the Sun that is not present in the planet's atmosphere
    B. the planet must be rotating
    C. some gas is present in the planet's atmosphere that is not present in the Sun
    D. some gas is present in the planet's atmosphere which is present in the Sun

23.____

24. The Earth's atmosphere is
    A. uniform in composition at all altitudes
    B. non-uniform, having the heaviest molecules at the lowest altitudes
    C. non-uniform, having variations in composition due to temperature and radiation
    D. non-uniform, having variations in composition due to decreasing escape velocity with altitude

24.____

25. The Moon's average temperature taken over a long period of time is
    A. somewhat lower than the Earth's average temperature
    B. equal to the Earth's average temperature
    C. somewhat higher than the Earth's average temperature
    D. undefinable because no atmosphere is present

25.____

KEY (CORRECT ANSWERS)

1.	A	11.	C
2.	B	12.	C
3.	A	13.	B
4.	B	14.	D
5.	D	15.	C
6.	B	16.	D
7.	B	17.	C
8.	C	18.	B
9.	A	19.	C
10.	B	20.	C

21. D
22. A
23. C
24. C
25. A

TEST 2

DIRECTIONS: Each question or incomplete statement is followed by several suggested answers or completions. Select the one that BEST answers the question or completes the statement. *PRINT THE LETTER OF THE CORRECT ANSWER IN THE SPACE AT THE RIGHT.*

1. The rotation of the Earth results in
   A. a tidal bulge
   B. an equatorial bulge
   C. a small motion of the north and south poles
   D. the shifting of the stars relative to one another

   1.____

2. The sidereal day is
   A. always slightly longer than the solar day
   B. always slightly shorter than the solar day
   C. equal in length to the solar day twice a year
   D. always equal to the solar day

   2.____

3. The "sidereal day" is defined as the interval between two successive transits of _____ across an observer's meridian.
   A. a star
   B. the Sun
   C. the Vernal Equinox
   D. the Moon

   3.____

4. On a day-to-day basis, the passage of time is determined from
   A. the position of the stars
   B. the position of the sun
   C. a highly accurate clock
   D. a theoretical analysis

   4.____

5. An eclipse can NEVER occur at the
   A. summer or winter solstice
   B. aphelion or perihelion of the Earth's orbit
   C. time when the Moon is near the line of nodes of the Earth-Moon orbit
   D. times of quadrature in the Moon's orbit

   5.____

6. The albedo of the Moon is
   A. the inclination of its orbit
   B. the fraction of light it reflects
   C. its average temperature
   D. the amount of sunlight it receives

   6.____

7. The path of totality in a solar eclipse is a narrow strip because the
   A. Moon is much smaller than the Sun
   B. Moon is smaller than the Earth
   C. umbra of the Moon's shadow barely reaches the Earth
   D. umbra of the Moon's shadow is a narrow strip

   7.____

8. An instantaneous photograph from a weather satellite of a solar eclipse on the Earth would show the zone of totality to be
   A. the whole Earth
   B. a round spot
   C. a narrow strip
   D. a circular ring

9. If the orbit of the Moon were in the ecliptic plane, we would observe during the course of one month
   A. one solar eclipse
   B. one lunar eclipse
   C. two lunar eclipses
   D. one solar and one lunar eclipse

10. During the total phase of a solar eclipse, the following CANNOT be seen:
    A. Corona
    B. Planets
    C. Sunspots
    D. Stars

11. A solar eclipse can NEVER be seen by
    A. an astronaut on the Moon
    B. an astronaut in orbit around the Earth
    C. both of the above
    D. none of the above

12. Suppose we had "ideal oceans" on the Earth's surface. High tides would be experienced when the Moon is
    A. only at the zenith (point directly overhead)
    B. at the zenith and nadir (point in sky opposite zenith)
    C. on the horizon
    D. none of the above

13. Observations of the tides in the solid Earth show it to be
    A. viscous, like an oily liquid
    B. slow in adjusting to tidal forces
    C. nearly instantaneous in response to tidal forces
    D. unaffected by tidal forces

14. At any location, the HIGHEST tides occur
    A. as a result of lunar action only
    B. as a result of solar action only
    C. at times when the centers of Earth, Moon, and Sun are nearly in line
    D. at times when the Moon is directly overhead

15. The Earth's non-spherical shape is MAINLY a result of
    A. the Earth's rotation
    B. tidal distortion
    C. perturbations caused by the planets
    D. the Earth's speed in its orbit

16. The tidal bulge on the Earth is always GREATEST
    A. in the plane of the Moon's orbit
    B. in the ecliptic plane (plane of the Earth's orbit)
    C. in the equator plane (plane of the Earth's equator)
    D. none of the above

17. The length of the day and of the month continually increase due MAINLY to
   A. perturbations
   B. aberration
   C. tidal friction
   D. seasonal effects

18. Hipparchus deduced from measurements of seasons
   A. solar rotation
   B. precession
   C. parallax of stars
   D. aberration

19. Which of the following has NOT been used to demonstrate rotation of the Earth?
   A. Foucault pendulum
   B. Foucault gyroscope
   C. Foucault knife edge
   D. Deviation of falling bodies

20. Suppose you were stationed in the crater Copernicus on the Moon. The Sun would rise
   A. each Earth day
   B. each Earth week
   C. each Earth month
   D. never

21. The MAXIMUM number of eclipses (lunar and solar) in a calendar year is
   A. two   B. four   C. five   D. seven

22. Suppose you were stationed on the crater Copernicus on the Moon. The Earth would set
   A. each Earth day
   B. each two weeks
   C. each month
   D. never

23. An observer studying the Moon over a period of several years would be able to see _____ of the Moon's surface.
   A. a quarter
   B. half
   C. more than half
   D. all

24. When earthshine is brightest on the Moon, the phase of the Earth as seen from the Moon is
   A. new
   B. first quarter
   C. full
   D. third quarter

25. If the moon revolved from east to west, the synodic month would be _____ the sidereal month.
   A. longer than
   B. shorter than
   C. the same as
   D. dependent upon

KEY (CORRECT ANSWERS)

1. B
2. B
3. C
4. C
5. D

6. B
7. C
8. B
9. D
10. C

11. D
12. B
13. C
14. C
15. A

16. A
17. C
18. B
19. C
20. C

21. D
22. D
23. C
24. C
25. B

TEST 3

DIRECTIONS: Each question or incomplete statement is followed by several suggested answers or completions. Select the one that BEST answers the question or completes the statement. *PRINT THE LETTER OF THE CORRECT ANSWER IN THE SPACE AT THE RIGHT.*

1. If the Earth were to speed up slightly in its orbit, so that a tropical year were completed in exactly 365 days, 3 hours, a leap year would be necessary each _____ years.
   A. four B. eight C. twelve D. sixteen

2. Since the mass of the Moon is $1/80^{th}$ that of the Earth, the center of mass of the Earth-Moon system is
   A. nearer to the Earth's center than to the Moon's center
   B. nearer to the Moon's center than to the Earth's center
   C. halfway between the two bodies
   D. at the Earth's center

3. A body raised high above the Earth's surface will weigh
   A. less than it would on the surface
   B. more than it would on the surface
   C. the same as it would on the surface
   D. none of the above

4. Stellar parallax, aberration, and retrograde motion are the result of the Earth's
   A. revolution around the Sun   B. rotation about its axis
   C. precession   D. nutation

5. In order to keep the seasons in step with the calendar, one employs the _____ year.
   A. sidereal B. tropical C. anomalistic D. martian

6. If one used the sidereal year as a basis for the calendar, the seasons would fall out of step with the calendar due to
   A. the Earth's eccentric orbit
   B. the Moon's gravitational influence
   C. precession of the equinoxes
   D. none of the above

7. The latitude of the north pole is
   A. 0° B. -90° C. +90° D. 360°

8. The Sun moves around the sky in a great circle which is called the
   A. celestial equator   B. zenith
   C. ecliptic pole   D. ecliptic

9. The sidereal period of a planet whose distance from the Sun is four astronomical units is _____ years.
   A. two   B. four   C. eight   D. sixteen

10. Over 99% of the mass of the solar system is concentrated in
    A. the Sun
    B. the planets
    C. comets and meteors
    D. none of the above

11. Aberration is caused by the
    A. inclination of the Earth's axis
    B. revolution of the Earth around the Sun
    C. shape of the Earth's orbit
    D. nonspherical shape of the Earth

12. The latitude of the equator is
    A. 0°   B. +90°   C. -90°   D. 180°

13. Seasons occur because of
    A. the rotation of the Earth
    B. the changing distance of the Earth from the Sun
    C. the tilt of the Earth's axis
    D. none of the above

14. The GREATEST amount of daylight in Ann Arbor, Michigan, occurs on
    A. March 21
    B. December 21
    C. June 21
    D. September 21

15. A total lunar eclipse is visible from _____ Earth.
    A. the entire
    B. a narrow strip on the
    C. a small circle on the
    D. the entire dark side of the

16. A body is dropped down a deep well at the north pole.
    A. Coriolis effect shifts it to the east.
    B. Coriolis effect shifts it to the west.
    C. Coriolis effect shifts it to the south.
    D. No shift due to Coriolis effect occurs.

17. Variation of latitude causes
    A. slight motion of the north celestial pole in the sky
    B. slight error in determination of a ship's position at sea
    C. slight error in the apparent positions of the planets relative to the stars
    D. motion of the air masses over the Earth

18. The aberration of starlight results in
    A. the apparent motion of stars in "orbits" about nothing
    B. the apparent motion of stars in "orbits" about stars very near to them
    C. an apparent motion of stars about the Sun
    D. bending of the light rays from stars

19. Is the sidereal day ever equal to the solar day in the course of a year? 19.____
    A. Yes
    B. Sometimes
    C. No
    D. During leap years

20. The duration of a second of time is derived from 20.____
    A. an extremely accurate clock
    B. the mean position of the Sun over a long period of time
    C. the mean position of the stars over a long period of time
    D. the mean position of the Moon over a long period of time

21. We have an extra day in leap year because the 21.____
    A. sidereal year is not equal to the tropical year
    B. tropical year is not an integral number of days
    C. sidereal year is not an integral number of days
    D. tropical year is affected by the precession of the equinoxes

22. Does an eclipse always occur when the moon is exactly on the line of nodes? 22.____
    A. Yes
    B. No
    C. Sometimes
    D. During sunspot activity

23. Is there a "Harvest Moon" effect in the spring? 23.____
    A. Yes, in the Northern Hemisphere only
    B. Yes, in the Southern Hemisphere only
    C. Never
    D. Always in both hemispheres

24. Baily's Beads are due to 24.____
    A. irregularities at the Sun's edge
    B. irregularities at the Moon's edge
    C. scintillation in the Earth's atmosphere
    D. the solar corona

25. During totality in a solar eclipse, we cannot see 25.____
    A. prominences on the Sun
    B. the corona of the Sun
    C. the surface of the Sun
    D. the surface of the Moon

KEY (CORRECT ANSWERS)

1.	B	11.	B
2.	A	12.	A
3.	A	13.	C
4.	A	14.	C
5.	B	15.	D
6.	C	16.	D
7.	C	17.	B
8.	D	18.	A
9.	C	19.	C
10.	A	20.	B

21. B
22. B
23. B
24. B
25. C

TEST 4

DIRECTIONS: Each question or incomplete statement is followed by several suggested answers or completions. Select the one that BEST answers the question or completes the statement. *PRINT THE LETTER OF THE CORRECT ANSWER IN THE SPACE AT THE RIGHT.*

1. The planets constitute APPROXIMATELY _____ mass of the solar system. 1._____
   A. the entire   B. 1/10 of the   C. 1/100 of the   D. 1/1000 of the

2. The mass of Venus is determined from 2._____
   A. the period and semi-major axis of its orbit around the Sun
   B. the observed acceleration it produces on one of its satellites
   C. perturbations in its orbit produced by nearby planets
   D. perturbations in the orbits of small bodies by Venus

3. The rotation of Jupiter is determined by measurement of 3._____
   A. perturbations in the orbits of its moon
   B. Doppler shifts in the radio emissions of the planet
   C. Doppler shifts in the sunlight reflected from the planet
   D. the precession of its polar axis

4. The key factors which control the nature of a planet's atmosphere are the molecular weights of gases and the planet's 4._____
   A. surface gravity and mean surface temperature
   B. surface gravity and albedo
   C. mean surface temperature and albedo
   D. surface gravity, mean surface temperature, and albedo

5. Which of these observed characteristics of Mercury indicates the possible presence of a thin atmosphere? 5._____
   A. The low albedo of the planet
   B. Absence of a twilight zone
   C. Considerable polarization of the light reflected from the planet
   D. Atmospheric absorption lines are absent from the light reflected from the planet

6. The retrograde rotation of Venus has been accurately measured through the use of radar. The method involves measuring 6._____
   A. radar radiation originating at fixed points on the planet's surface
   B. the effect radar signals from Earth have on the planet's atmosphere
   C. radar signals from Earth reflected by fixed features on the planet's surface
   D. radar radiation originating in the sun reflected by fixed features on the planet's surface

2 (#4)

7. The transition from winter to summer on Mars is marked by _____ of the southern polar cap and _____ of the maria.
   A. decrease; darkening
   B. decrease; lightening
   C. increase; darkening
   D. increase; lightening

   7.____

8. The "red spot" on Jupiter is a
   A. transient cloud of vast size photographed in 1931
   B. permanent fixed feature of the planet
   C. permanent but variable feature of the planet
   D. wandering feature of constant size and color

   8.____

9. Saturn's rings are not a solid sheet of material. Which of the following is NOT a proof of this?
   A. When viewed edge on, they cannot be discerned.
   B. Stars can be seen through the rings.
   C. Doppler shifts in the spectrum of light reflected by the rings show the inside rotating faster than the outside.
   D. Cassini's division occurs at a distance where particles would be perturbed severely by the satellite Mimas.

   9.____

10. Uranus differs markedly from the other "gas giants" in
    A. its albedo
    B. its period of rotation
    C. the inclination of its axis
    D. the eccentricity of its orbit

    10.____

11. The gas giants – Jupiter, Saturn, Uranus, and Neptune – are considerably
    A. more massive and denser
    B. more massive but less dense
    C. less massive but denser
    D. less massive and less dense

    11.____

12. Venus and Earth are a pair of planets similar to each other EXCEPT for
    A. period of rotation
    B. diameter
    C. mass
    D. inclination of axes

    12.____

13. Jupiter and Saturn are a pair of planets similar to each other EXCEPT for
    A. period of rotation
    B. diameter
    C. mass
    D. color

    13.____

14. Uranus and Neptune are a pair of planets similar to each other. They differ significantly from Jupiter and Saturn in diameter, mass, and
    A. period of rotation
    B. color
    C. eccentricity of orbit
    D. internal structure

    14.____

15. Which one of the following is NOT true of Neptune?
    A. One of its moons moves backwards in its orbit.
    B. One of its moons has the highest eccentricity of any satellite.
    C. It does not fit in the planetary positions predicted.
    D. It is the most oblate planet.

    15.____

3 (#4)

16. Pluto's rotation period is obtained by
    A. observation of surface features over a long period
    B. measurement of Doppler shift in the sunlight reflected by the planet
    C. observation of variations of the planet's brightness
    D. fluctuations in radio emission from the planet

16.____

17. Which of the following is NOT true of the minor planets?
    A. They generally have highly eccentric orbits.
    B. The largest is almost 500 miles in diameter.
    C. Estimates of their numbers exceed 40,000.
    D. Most of them have orbits of low inclination.

17.____

18. The mass of a minor planet is obtained from
    A. perturbations in its orbit produced by large planets
    B. the period and semi-major axis of its orbit
    C. its estimated size and assumed density
    D. its period of rotation and estimated size

18.____

19. Bode's Law indicates a planetary position that is occupied by some of the minor planets. The estimated combined mass of all the minor planets is
    A. almost that of Jupiter   B. about $1/3$ that of the Earth
    C. about $1/20$ that of the Moon   D. about $1/1600$ that of the Moon

19.____

20. Which of the planets have two known natural satellites?
    A. Mars and Uranus   B. Mars and Neptune
    C. Mars, Uranus, and Neptune D. Mars alone

20.____

21. The D, E, F1, and F2 layers in the Earth's atmosphere are concentrations of
    A. ozone molecules   B. hydrogen atoms
    C. ionized oxygen and nitrogen atoms   D. charged dust particles

21.____

22. Which of the following is NOT a proof of the lack of a thin lunar atmosphere?
    A. Absence of a twilight zone
    B. Presence of numerous craters
    C. Sudden blinking out of a star during occultation by the Moon
    D. Sudden drop in temperature of most of the surface during an eclipse of the Moon

22.____

23. The large lunar maria are
    A. younger than the adjacent craters
    B. the same age as the adjacent craters
    C. older than the adjacent craters
    D. of indeterminant relative age

23.____

24. Craters on the Moon are generally believed to be
    A. volcanic in origin
    B. the result of meteoritic impact explosions
    C. formed by geological forces when the crust formed
    D. any of the above, depending on individual circumstances

25. The Earth's magnetic field is probably due to
    A. large amounts of magnetized iron in the semi-molten core
    B. rapid rotation of magnetized iron in the semi-molten mantle
    C. electrical currents generated by rotation in the semi-molten mantle
    D. electrical currents generated by rotation in the semi-molten core

KEY (CORRECT ANSWERS)

1.	D	11.	B
2.	D	12.	A
3.	C	13.	C
4.	A	14.	B
5.	C	15.	D
6.	C	16.	C
7.	A	17.	A
8.	C	18.	C
9.	A	19.	C
10.	C	20.	B

21.	C
22.	B
23.	A
24.	B
25.	D

TEST 5

DIRECTIONS: Each question or incomplete statement is followed by several suggested answers or completions. Select the one that BEST answers the question or completes the statement. *PRINT THE LETTER OF THE CORRECT ANSWER IN THE SPACE AT THE RIGHT.*

1. The EARLIEST existing astronomical records are   1._____
   A. Chinese   B. Egyptian   C. Greek   D. Arabic

2. The Sun moves with respect to the stars   2._____
   A. west-east only
   B. north-south only
   C. west-east rapidly, north-south slowly
   D. erratically

3. Greek astronomy was practiced CHIEFLY in   3._____
   A. Greece   B. Egypt   C. Arabia   D. Mesopotamia

4. The Sun appears to rise in the _____ part of the sky.   4._____
   A. eastern   B. southern   C. western   D. northern

5. How many moving astronomical objects can be seen regularly without a telescope?   5._____
   A. Two   B. Four   C. Seven   D. Eleven

6. Constellations are   6._____
   A. clusters of stars   B. bright stars
   C. groups of planets   D. areas of the sky

7. The apparent form of the Moon as seen in the sky depends on   7._____
   A. how much of the Moon's daylight hemisphere is visible
   B. the rate of rotation of the Moon
   C. the rate of revolution of the Moon
   D. the motion of the Earth

8. At first quarter, the Moon has the shape of a   8._____
   A. quarter-circle   B. half-circle
   C. crescent   D. rectangle

9. The words *new, crescent, first quarter, full, gibbous, third quarter,* ALL describe lunar   9._____
   A. mountains   B. eclipses   C. phases   D. tides

10. An observation, known to Aristotle, in support of the spherical shape of the Earth, is the
    A. shape of shadow of the Earth on the Moon during a lunar eclipse
    B. phases of the Moon
    C. rotation of the Earth
    D. alternation of seasons

    10.____

11. Aristarchus' principal astronomical measurement was
    A. relative size of system Earth-Moon-Sun
    B. stellar parallax
    C. rotation of the Earth
    D. obliquity of ecliptic

    11.____

12. Eratosthenes' principal astronomical measurement was
    A. size of Moon   B. planetary distances
    C. size of Earth   D. planetary periods

    12.____

13. Planets generally move with respect to the stellar background
    A. not at all   B. from west to east
    C. from east to west   D. in undetermined fashion

    13.____

14. Temporary planetary motion from east to west for short intervals of time is called
    A. precession   B. rotation
    C. dispersion   D. retrograde

    14.____

15. What percentage fraction of the total area of the sky is visible to an observer located on the Earth's equator?
    A. 10%   B. 25%   C. 50%   D. 100%

    15.____

16. Which of the following systems is geocentric?
    A. Solar system   B. Jupiter's satellite system
    C. Saturn's satellite system   D. Earth-Moon system

    16.____

17. Copernicus based his theories on observations by
    A. himself
    B. Greek astronomers
    C. Arabian astronomers
    D. combinations of Greek and Arabian astronomers

    17.____

18. A planet that is farther from the Sun than the Earth is called a _____ planet.
    A. superior   b. inferior   C. minor   D. Copernican

    18.____

19. A superior planet may be observed BEST at
    A. inferior conjunction   B. quadrature
    C. noon   D. opposition

    19.____

20. An inferior planet may be observed BEST at 20.____
    A. inferior conjunction   B. greatest elongation
    C. noon   D. superior conjunction

21. One pair of the following named planets are inferior planets. Which pair? 21.____
    A. Saturn, Jupiter   B. Mercury, Venus
    C. Mars, Venus   D. Saturn, Mercury

22. The period of revolution of a planet around the sun from a star to the same 22.____
    star again, as seen from the Sun, is the _____ period.
    A. synodic   B. sidereal   C. harmonic   D. natural

23. The interval between two successive times when a planet occupies the 23.____
    same position in relation to the Sun as seen from the Earth is called the_____
    period.
    A. synodic   B. sidereal   C. harmonic   D. natural

24. To derive the relative distance of the planets, which of the following 24.____
    quantities need NOT be known?
    A. Sidereal period   B. Synodic period
    C. Angles of elongation at two times   D. Brightness

25. Tycho Brahe gained his principal reputation as a(n) 25.____
    A. observing astronomer   B. mathematician
    C. physicist   D. cosmogonist

KEY (CORRECT ANSWERS)

1.	A	11.	A
2.	C	12.	C
3.	B	13.	B
4.	A	14.	D
5.	C	15.	D
6.	D	16.	D
7.	A	17.	D
8.	B	18.	A
9.	C	19.	D
10.	A	20.	B

21. B
22. B
23. A
24. D
25. A

ASTRONOMY

EXAMINATION SECTION
TEST 1

DIRECTIONS: Each question or incomplete statement is followed by several suggested answers or completions. Select the one that BEST answers the question or completes the statement. *PRINT THE LETTER OF THE CORRECT ANSWER IN THE SPACE AT THE RIGHT.*

1. Kepler's GREATEST contributions to astronomy are

    A. music of the spheres
    B. optical theory
    C. tables of planets
    D. three laws of planetary motion

    1._____

2. Which of the following is NOT a property of an ellipse?

    A. Plane curve
    B. Has two foci
    C. sum of the distances from the two foci to any point on the curves is constant
    D. The center of the ellipse is the same distance from all points of the curve

    2._____

3. Kepler's FIRST LAW was deduced from observation of

    A. all planets   B. Mars only
    C. the inferior planets   D. Sun and Mars

    3._____

4. Kepler's SECOND LAW is based on the following:

    A. Mars moves fastest when closest to the sun
    B. Properties of the ellipse
    C. Retrograde motions
    D. Mars' period of revolution

    4._____

5. Kepler's THIRD LAW resulted from a search for

    A. underlying harmony in nature
    B. gravitational forces
    C. a method of measuring planetary distances
    D. a method of improving planetary periods

    5._____

6. Kepler revised the estimated distance to the sun. His revision was based on

    A. his three laws   B. direct measurement
    C. no direct evidence   D. no diurnal parallax for Mars

    6._____

7. One of the following was an astronomical discovery NOT made by Galileo with a telescope. Indicate the correct one.

    A. Phases of Venus   B. Spots on the sun
    C. Mountains on the moon   D. Faculae on the sun

    7._____

8. Rockets and jets operate on the principle of

   A. Newton's FIRST LAW
   B. Newton's SECOND LAW
   C. Newton's THIRD LAW
   D. Universal Law of Gravitation

9. On the surface of the earth, Neil Armstrong weighs 180 pounds, whereas on the surface of the moon he weighs 30 pounds. The reason for this is:

   A. He is less massive on the moon.
   B. The moon is more massive than the earth.
   C. The moon has no atmosphere.
   D. The moon is less massive than the earth.

10. When dropped from the same height, a cannon ball and a marble strike the earth's surface at the same time. This is TRUE because

    A. the mass of the marble and the cannon ball are the same
    B. the weight of the marble and the cannon ball are the same
    C. the acceleration of the marble and the cannon ball are the same
    D. the gravitational force on the marble and the cannon ball are the same

11. The number of meteoritic impact craters known on the earth is

    A. two
    B. several dozen
    C. several hundred
    D. several thousand

12. Mercury rotates in such a way that the same side faces the sun

    A. at all times
    B. at successive perihelions
    C. at alternate perihelions
    D. on every third perihelion

13. Which of the following is NOT a proof that Venus has a significant atmosphere?

    A. Its measured temperature is different at different wavelengths.
    B. It reflects 75% of the sunlight striking it.
    C. The points of its crescent extend more than half way around the planetary disc.
    D. The spectrum of light reflected from it has lines in it not in the solar spectrum

14. The "canals" on Mars seen by observers on earth have

    A. been observed by the Mariner IV space probe
    B. not been observed by Mariner IV, and are thought to be an optical illusion
    C. not been observed by Mariner IV because it did not look at regions supposedly having "canals"
    D. not been observed by Mariner IV because it was specially equipped with filters to show craters, not "canals"

15. Which of the following is NOT true of Jupiter?

    A. It has two satellites, Ganymede and Callisto, larger than the earth's moon.
    B. It has a magnetic field and "Van Allen" belts.
    C. Its atmosphere consists mainly of hydrogen, helium, carbon dioxide, methane, and ammonia.
    D. Its atmosphere is probably not more than several hundred miles thick.

16. Saturn's rings MOST probably formed

    A. when the planet itself formed
    B. over billions of years as the planet "captured" such material
    C. when a comet was perturbed into that orbit around the planet
    D. when a moon moved closer to the planet than Roche's limit

17. Which of the following is NOT true of Pluto?

    A. Its orbit has the highest inclination of any planet.
    B. Its orbit has the greatest eccentricity of any planet.
    C. It is smaller than Mars in diameter and mass.
    D. One of its moons moves backwards in its orbit.

18. A meteor shower radiant, seen against the celestial sphere, is

    A. the angle from the zenith of the convergent point of the meteor tracks
    B. the small region from which the meteor tracks radiate
    C. the great circle to which all meteor tracks are parallel
    D. the center of the large circle which defines the region of the meteor shower

19. The ages of meteorites, measured by radioactive dating, are

    A. considerably younger than the age of the earth
    B. about the same as the age of the earth
    C. considerably older than the age of the earth
    D. various, some younger and some older

20. Which of the following is NOT true of comets?

    A. They probably have a rocky or metallic core.
    B. The greater part of their substance is in the form of ices which sublime as they approach the sun.
    C. Cometary masses are known from the perturbation they produce on asteroids and satellites of planets.
    D. Comets have been measured near the sun with temperatures as high as 4500°K.

21. The age of the earth is derived from studies of the radioactivity of surface rocks. A rock's radioactive "life" as measured this way begins

    A. in the primordial "fireball" -- the beginning of the universe
    B. when the solar system formed from dust and gas
    C. when the rock solidified from the liquid magma which formed the primitive planet (earth)
    D. when the rock was last exposed to strong atomic radiation from the new formed sun

22. Which of the following is NOT primarily due to atomic particles in the earth's magnetic field?

    A. The aurora borealis (Northern lights)
    B. The solar wind
    C. Static in ordinary radio transmission
    D. The Van Allen belts

23. Primary evidence that the moon's core has solidified is the

    A. absence of lunar seismic activity
    B. lower average temperature of the surface compared to the earth
    C. lack of a lunar magnetic field
    D. large variation of temperature on the surface

24. There are fewer large craters in the moon's maria because

    A. the maria remained molten much longer than other areas after the moon formed
    B. the maria consist of a material that does not form craters easily
    C. the maria are of more recent origin and insufficient time has passed for many large object collisions
    D. the maria are of more recent origin and large object collisions in the solar system no longer occur

25. The light colored streaks radiating out from the crater Copernicus indicate that

    A. the material underneath the surface was lighter colored than the surface
    B. the material underneath the surface was darker colored than the surface
    C. the impact explosion produced a chemical change in the ejected material which lightened its color
    D. blast burning of surface material occurred in the impact explosion, producing the streaks

KEY (CORRECT ANSWERS)

1. D		11. B	
2. D		12. C	
3. D		13. A	
4. A		14. B	
5. A		15. C	
6. D		16. D	
7. D		17. D	
8. C		18. B	
9. D		19. B	
10. C		20. C	

21. C
22. B
23. A
24. C
25. A

TEST 2

DIRECTIONS: Each question or incomplete statement is followed by several suggested answers or completions. Select the one that BEST answers the question or completes the statement. *PRINT THE LETTER OF THE CORRECT ANSWER IN THE SPACE AT THE RIGHT.*

1. Perturbations of the orbit of Uranus lead to the discovery of
   A. Halley's comet
   B. Neptune
   C. Titan
   D. Jupiter

   1.____

2. Consider a minor planet in a circular orbit about 4 times as far from the sun as is the earth. The orbital period of this minor planet is
   A. 4 years
   B. 8 years
   C. 16 years
   D. 64 years

   2.____

3. Suppose the earth were twice as far from the sun as it is now. The sun's attractive force on the earth would then be _____ as great as now.
   A. 1/2
   B. 1/4
   C. 1/8
   D. 1/16

   3.____

4. One way to reduce environmental pollution on the earth would be to send all industrial wastes into the sun. In order to send a spaceship directly to the sun, it MUST be launched
   A. from the equator at local noon on March 21 or September 22
   B. in the direction of the earth's motion at the escape velocity of about 7 miles/second
   C. opposite to the direction of the earth's orbital motion at the escape velocity of 7 miles/second
   D. opposite to the direction of the earth's orbital motion at the earth's orbital velocity of about 18.5 miles/second

   4.____

5. The mass of the earth can be measured by
   A. comparing the attraction between the earth and a given mass, M_A, to the attraction between another mass, M_B, and M_A
   B. multiplying the density of a small sample of the surface of the earth by the volume of the earth
   C. measuring the altitude of stars from different, known positions on the earth
   D. none of the above

   5.____

6. How long will it take a space probe to go from the Earth to Jupiter on a minimum energy transfer orbit? The semi-major axis of Jupiter's orbit is about 5 AU, and of the Earth's orbit is 1 AU.
   A. $\frac{1}{2}(4^{3/2})$ year
   B. $3^{3/2}$ year
   C. $\frac{1}{2}(3^{3/2})$ year
   D. $\frac{1}{2}(6^{3/2})$ year

   6.____

7. How much would a 100-pound person weigh on Jupiter? The mass of Jupiter is about 300 times that of the Earth, and its radius is about 11 times that of the Earth. G is the gravitational constant.

   7.____

A. $\dfrac{100 \times 300}{(11)}$ lb.
B. $\dfrac{100 \times 300}{(11)^2}$ lb.
C. $\dfrac{100 \times G \times 300}{(11)^2}$ lb.
D. $\dfrac{100 \times G \times 300 \times 100}{(11)^2}$ lb.

8. One of the proofs that the earth revolves about the sun is   8.____

   A. diurnal motion
   B. the annual motion of the sun
   C. the aberration of starlight
   D. the behavior of a Foucault pendulum

9. Why isn't Venus always exactly behind the sun at superior conjunction?   9.____

   A. Its period is too long.
   B. It is always exactly behind the sun at superior conjunction.
   C. It is never behind the sun at superior conjunction.
   D. Its orbital plane is inclined to the ecliptic.

10. As seen from the earth, the moon appears to move about _____ with respect to the stars.   10.____

    A. 1° per day
    B. 13° per day
    C. 24° per day
    D. none of the above

11. If the speed of an object in a circular orbit around the earth is V mi/hr, then its speed would have to increase to at least _____ in order to escape from the earth.   11.____

    A. $\sqrt{2}$ V mi/hr
    B. 2 V mi/hr
    C. Neither of these
    D. Not enough information

12. Ariel is a satellite of the planet Uranus. It is about 1/2 as far from the center of Uranus as the Moon is from the center of the Earth, and its orbital period is about 1/10 that of the Moon about the Earth. Using this data, what is the ratio of the mass of Uranus plus Ariel to the mass of the Earth plus the Moon?   12.____

    A. 4/1000   B. 8/100   C. 100/8   D. 1000/4

13. The Greeks had to adopt models for the motions of the planets that were more complex than uniform motion in circles centered on the earth because this simple model   13.____

    A. conflicted with their religious views
    B. did not explain the synodic periods of the planets
    C. did not explain retrograde motion
    D. none of the above

14. A body falling freely in a gravitational field has   14.____

    A. constant velocity
    B. constant acceleration
    C. neither of the above
    D. both of the above

15. What is the eccentricity of the orbit of a planet whose perihelion distance is 1 AU and whose aphelion distance is 3 AU?

    A. 1/4 B. 3/2 C. 1/2 D. 4

16. As seen from the north ecliptic pole, which of the following statements is TRUE?

    A. The orbital motions of the inferior planets are counter-clockwise and of the superior planets are clockwise.
    B. The orbital motions of the superior planets are counter-clockwise and of the inferior planets are clockwise.
    C. The orbital motions of all the planets are counterclockwise.
    D. The orbital motions of all the planets are clockwise.

17. Suppose Aristarchus had found that the interval from the first quarter moon to third quarter moon was the same as from the third quarter to the first. He would have concluded that

    A. the sun and moon were equally distant from the earth
    B. the sun was infinitely far away
    C. the moon was infinitely far away
    D. the sun was $\sqrt{2}$ times as far from the earth as the moon

18. Copernicus determined the distances of inferior planets from the sun (in terms of the earth's distance from the sun) by observing the planet at

    A. quadrature
    B. inferior conjunction
    C. superior conjunction
    D. greatest elongation

19. If at sunrise the moon were setting for an observer in northern Michigan, the phase of the moon would be

    A. new B. first quarter C. full D. last quarter

20. Suppose you observed that a particular star was 20° above the horizon when it was on the meridian. After taking 10^6 steps due north, you observed that this star was only 10° above the horizon when it was on the meridian. What is the circumference of the planet you are on? (Assume the planet is spherical.)

    A. 18×10^6 steps
    B. 36×10^6 steps
    C. 369×10^6 steps
    D. 7200×10^6 steps

21. The polar axis of a telescope

    A. always points toward the observer's zenith
    B. is always set parallel to the axis of rotation of the earth
    C. is oriented the same, relative to the ground, at all observatories
    D. is parallel to the telescope's other axis, the declination axis

22. When moonshine is brightest on the earth, what must be the phase of the earth, as seen from the moon?

    A. New B. First quarter C. Full D. Last quarter

23. The solar spectrum observed at the earth is

    A. a bright line (emission) spectrum superimposed on a continuous spectrum
    B. a dark line (absorption) spectrum superimposed on a continuous spectrum
    C. a continuous spectrum only
    D. both A and B

24. The accepted age of Stonehenge was recently increased by about 800 years. This change came about because it is thought now that the carbon-14 method of dating organic material gives results that are

    A. in error due to variations in the rate of production of carbon 14 in the past
    B. in error due to variations in the decay rate of carbon 14 from sample to sample
    C. in error due to inaccurate measuring techniques
    D. carbon-14 has nothing to do with it; the Druids were discovered to have lived earlier than was previously thought

25. The solar day (24 hours of solar time) is slightly shorter than the sidereal day (24 hours of sidereal time).

    A. Always   B. Never   C. Sometimes   D. Relative

KEYS (CORRECT ANSWERS)

1. B	11. A
2. B	12. C
3. B	13. C
4. D	14. B
5. A	15. C
6. C	16. C
7. B	17. B
8. C	18. D
9. D	19. C
10. B	20. B

21. B
22. A
23. B
24. A
25. B

TEST 3

DIRECTIONS: Each question or incomplete statement is followed by several suggested answers or completions. Select the one that BEST answers the question or completes the statement. *PRINT THE LETTER OF THE CORRECT ANSWER IN THE SPACE AT THE RIGHT.*

1. Apparent solar days are NOT of uniform duration throughout the year because 1.____

    A. the earth's rotation rate is speeding up
    B. the earth's axis is not perpendicular to the plane of the earth's orbit
    C. the earth's orbital speed is faster at perihelion than at aphelion
    D. both B and C

2. Suppose you were in a ship sailing east and you cross the International Date Line. Before you cross it, the standard time (zone time) is 9:45 Monday morning. What are the standard time and day 15 minutes later after you cross the line? 2.____

    A. 10 a.m. Sunday
    B. 11 a.m. Sunday
    C. 9 a.m. Tuesday
    D. 10 a.m. Tuesday

3. Assuming Newton's laws of mechanics are correct, the Fou-cault pendulum experiment 3.____

    A. is a definite proof that the earth rotates
    B. is fun to look at but does not tell us anything
    C. does not show the earth's rotation at the pole
    D. works well to demonstrate the earth's rotation at the equator

4. Right ascension and declination, which are based on an extension of the earth's axis of rotation and equatorial plane onto the celestial sphere, form a practical coordinate system because 4.____

    A. the definitions are easy to remember
    B. the coordinates of a fixed point on the celestial sphere, e.g., a star, are not changed by the earth's rotation
    C. the coordinates of a fixed point on the celestial sphere change constantly due to the earth's rotation
    D. Polaris is near the pole and another bright star is near the Vernal Equinox

5. The equation of time 5.____

    A. is difficult to solve since it is an n-th order polynomial with constant coefficients
    B. is Newton's form of Kepler's second law (equal areas)
    C. is a relation that gives the obliquity of the ecliptic of any date
    D. is the amount by which the fictitious (mean) and true (apparent) sun differ in their positions in the sky

6. A blackbody has a _____ type of spectrum. 6.____

    A. line emission
    B. band emission
    C. continuous emission
    D. line absorption

7. Telescope A: A reflector with a 30-inch aperture objective of 150-inch focal length and an eyepiece of 2-inch focal length

   Telescope B: A refractor with a 10-inch aperture objective of 150-inch focal length and an eyepiece of 1-inch focal length

   Which statement below is FALSE?

   A. A has better resolving power than B.
   B. B has greater magnification than A.
   C. Point sources will be brighter in B.
   D. Extended sources will be brighter in A.

8. How can the mid-summer sunrise be directly over the heel-stone at Stonehenge now even though the stone has tilted since the monument was built 40 centuries ago?

   A. Planetary precession has caused the apparent position of sunrise to shift enough to compensate for the change in position of the top of the stone.
   B. Luni-solar precession has caused the time of the midsummer sunrise to change enough to compensate for the change in position of the top of the stone.
   C. The Druids are the only ones to observe the sunrise, and their reports are not to be trusted.
   D. The mid-summer sunrise did not take place over the heelstone when the monument was built.

9. Atmospheric refraction makes a star's altitude appear less than it really is.

   A. True   B. False   C. Sometimes   D. Relative

10. Which of the following is MOST closely related to the fact that the moon appears dimly red during many total lunar eclipses?

    A. "Earthshine"
    B. Diffraction of light near the earth's edge
    C. Refraction of light by the earth's atmosphere
    D. Infrared radiation from the moon

11. If the temperature of a blackbody were doubled, the rate at which it radiates energy would increase by a factor of _____.

    A. $2^{2/3}$ B. 2 C. $2^{3/2}$ D. 2^4

12. If the earth and the moon were farther from the sun (but the earth-moon distance remained constant), then

    A. solar eclipses would occur more often
    B. solar eclipses would occur less often
    C. solar eclipses would be visible over a larger area of the earth
    D. both A and D

13. Would a company whose goal was to make a perpetual motion machine be a good investment?

A. Yes, since everyone likes to get something for nothing, such a machine would sell well.
B. Yes, such a machine would end worries about running out of energy sources on the earth.
C. No, according to our experience, summarized in the second law of thermodynamics, it is not possible to build such a machine.
D. No, such a machine would not be beneficial because it would be too hard to control; there would be no way to stop it.

14. The harvest moon is caused by

    A. the inclination of the celestial equator to the horizon
    B. the inclination of the moon's orbit to the ecliptic
    C. the autumnal equinox
    D. the clear skies in the fall

15. You are aboard a ship which is hijacked by pirates who leave you stranded on a desert island. You must send a message for help by bottle, but you do not know where you are. You have a watch that gives you Greenwich time and you see that at night the north star is about 1/4 of the way between the horizon and the zenith (but closer to the horizon than the zenith). Can you estimate your location?

    A. No, not enough information
    B. Yes, 5^h east longitude, $23°$ north latitude
    C. Yes, 5^h east longitude, $23°$ south latitude
    D. Yes, 5^h west longitude, $23°$ north latitude

16. Spectra of Jupiter show strong absorption due to ammonia. This absorption is not present in spectra of Saturn. It is thought that this is due to

    A. Saturn's being so cold that the ammonia would be frozen on the surface of the planet
    B. Saturn's not having any ammonia
    C. Saturn's rotating so fast that the ammonia lines are so broad that they cannot be recognized
    D. the ammonia lines of Saturn being hidden by absorption due to ammonia in the earth's atmosphere

17. A similarity between the rings of Saturn and the minor planet zone is

    A. their location
    B. the orbital periods of the particles in them
    C. the size distribution of the particles in them
    D. the existence of gaps or regions where there are very few particles

18. Long-period comets generally have their orbital planes nearly coincident with the ecliptic plane.

    A. True   B. False
    C. Sometimes   D. Not enough information given

19. Short-period comets were

    A. long-period comets whose orbits decayed by interaction with the solar wind
    B. long-period comets that were perturbed by stars into short-period orbits
    C. long-period comets that were perturbed by the planets into short-period orbits
    D. formed in their present, short-period orbits

20. The accretion theory for the origin of the comets implies that

    A. comets are formed in long-period orbits of high eccentricity
    B. comets are formed in long-period orbits of low eccentricity
    C. comets are formed of material left over from the formation of the solar system
    D. we will eventually run out of comets

21. The period of rotation of Mercury is now thought to be 2/3 of its orbital period. This recent value for the period of rotation is due to

    A. extensive visual observations
    B. extensive radar observations
    C. information returned by mariner spacecraft
    D. none of the above

22. The atmosphere of Venus appears to be MOSTLY

    A. water vapor
    B. oxygen
    C. nitrogen
    D. carbon dioxide

23. Not much is known about the surface of Venus because the planet

    A. is rotating too fast to photograph the surface
    B. is too close to the sun
    C. has a cloudy atmosphere
    D. is too far away to resolve the surface features

24. Meteorites are all so small that they are not capable of damaging areas on the earth as large as a city block.

    A. True
    B. False
    C. Not until the present time
    D. Unknown

25. The _____ of at least some meteorites indicate that they were once part of planet-sized objects.

    A. sizes
    B. masses
    C. internal structures
    D. orbits

KEY (CORRECT ANSWERS)

1.	D	11.	D
2.	D	12.	D
3.	A	13.	C
4.	B	14.	B
5.	D	15.	A
6.	C	16.	A
7.	C	17.	D
8.	A	18.	B
9.	B	19.	C
10.	C	20.	A

21. B
22. D
23. C
24. B
25. C

TEST 4

DIRECTIONS: Each question or incomplete statement is followed by several suggested answers or completions. Select the one that BEST answers the question or completes the statement. *PRINT THE LETTER OF THE CORRECT ANSWER IN THE SPACE AT THE RIGHT.*

1. The temperature of a planet is determined by the _____ between the energy received from the sun (minus that reflected) and the energy radiated by the planet.

   A. balance
   B. interference
   C. compensation
   D. none of these

2. The Roche limit is

   A. the limiting brightness which the eye can detect
   B. the limiting distance inside which large solid bodies would be destroyed by tidal forces
   C. the zone inside which rapidly moving charged particles are trapped in the earth's magnetic field
   D. the limit at which solar energy vaporizes

3. The gegenshine is

   A. a meteor shower
   B. a flow of light opposite the sun
   C. the upper part (above 50 miles) of the earth's atmosphere
   D. interior crust of the lunar surface

4. Upper limits have been placed on the masses of comets using

   A. perturbation theory
   B. estimates of comets' dimensions
   C. Kepler's Third Law
   D. Galileo's First Hypothesis

5. One of the major consequences of the theory that the planetary system arose as a natural result of the formation of the sun is that

   A. it removes the angular momentum difficulty
   B. it shows that Kepler's laws are valid elsewhere
   C. it implies that there are probably planets around other stars
   D. it proves the theories of the evolution of life

6. It is thought that life could have originated spontaneously on the primitive earth provided there was (were)

   A. a reducing (hydrogen rich) atmosphere
   B. water
   C. energy in the form of lightning or ultraviolet light
   D. all of these

7. The MAIN reason for believing there is probably not intelligent life on Mars is that

   A. we have not seen it
   B. it has not contacted us
   C. there is too little water on Mars
   D. it is too cold on Mars

8. One objection to the idea that the moon was captured by the earth is that the temperatures of the surfaces of the earth and the moon would have been raised to the melting point of rock, but no evidence has been found that this occurred. This objection has recently been removed

   A. by noting that a resonance between the rotation of the earth and the revolution of the moon would prevent such strong heating
   B. by noting that the age of the moon is much less than formerly thought
   C. by interpreting the peculiar glazing phenomenon found by the Apollo 11 astronauts on lunar rocks as evidence that such strong heating did occur
   D. by discovering that the moon really came from the crust of the earth from what is now the Pacific Ocean

9. Which of the following CAN be used to determine the relative ages of lunar features?

   A. Overlap of features
   B. Number of craters per unit area
   C. Sharpness of craters
   D. All of these

10. Is it likely that there are bright aurora on Mars as there are on the Earth?

    A. Yes
    B. No
    C. Maybe
    D. Cannot be determined

11. It now seems that the canals on Mars are

    A. irrigation ditches
    B. more or less linear arrangements of craters
    C. dark dust blown by the prevailing winds
    D. inexplicable

12. Of the following, the STRONGEST evidence that the south pole cap of Mars is frozen carbon dioxide is

    A. the temperature of the cap is that expected for frozen carbon dioxide
    B. the color is that of frozen carbon dioxide
    C. no rivers of water are seen leading away from the cap
    D. it is probably not frozen carbon dioxide

13. The rotation rate of Jupiter has been determined MOST accurately by

    A. radar
    B. doppler shift in visible spectra
    C. timing the passage of features in the cloud belts across the central meridian of the planet
    D. measuring the oblateness of the planet

14. The evidence that Jupiter and Saturn are MOSTLY hydrogen is   14.____

    A. their large size
    B. their large mass
    C. their light color
    D. their low density

15. The MOST recently discovered satellite of Saturn, its tenth, was predicted by   15.____

    A. studying the structure of the ring system
    B. applying Bode's Law to Saturn's satellites
    C. noting that 10 is an even number but 9 is an odd number
    D. Albert Einstein

16. The fact that Venus, Mars and the Moon have vanishingly small magnetic fields, while the   16.____
    Earth and Jupiter have strong magnetic fields implies that

    A. magnetic fields are a property of all rotating bodies
    B. in order to have a strong magnetic field, a planet must rotate rapidly
    C. in order to have a strong magnetic field, a planet must have a mass of the same order as that of the earth or larger
    D. both B and C

17. The oblateness of Jupiter and Saturn is caused by   17.____

    A. their distance from the sun
    B. their extensive system of satellites
    C. their thick cloud layers
    D. their rapid rotation

18. MOST of the minor planets have orbits whose semi-major axes are about   18.____

    A. 1 AU   B. 1.5 AU   C. 3 AU   D. 5 AU

19. The Trojans are NOT   19.____

    A. between the orbits of Jupiter and Mars
    B. 60° from Jupiter as seen from the sun
    C. an example of a special solution of the three-body problem
    D. minor planets

20. Comets always have tails.   20.____

    A. True   B. False   C. True so far   D. Unknown

21. A comet tail that is relatively straight and blue is probably a tail of   21.____

    A. type I (ionized gases)
    B. type II (dust)
    C. type III (water)
    D. none of the above

22. A meteor shower results from   22.____

    A. a statistical fluctuation (concentration) in the random arrival of interplanetary particles
    B. observing in the hours after midnight
    C. the earth's passing through the orbit of a comet
    D. passing through a geophysical phenomenon

23. The meteors after midnight are more spectacular than before midnight because

   A. the particles collide head-on with the earth
   B. the orbital speed of the earth is greater
   C. the particles are bigger
   D. the particles catch up with the earth

24. The day on Mars is _____ as the day on earth.

   A. less than half as long
   B. about the same length
   C. more than twice as long
   D. three times as long

25. The planets (including the minor planets) are the only objects in the solar system whose spacing is given approximately by "Bode's Law" or by a rule which is similar to Bode's Law.

   A. True   B. False   C. True so far   D. Unknown

KEY (CORRECT ANSWERS)

1.	A		11.	B
2.	B		12.	A
3.	B		13.	C
4.	A		14.	D
5.	C		15.	A
6.	D		16.	D
7.	C		17.	D
8.	A		18.	C
9.	D		19.	A
10.	B		20.	B

21. A
22. C
23. A
24. B
25. B

ASTRONOMY
EXAMINATION SECTION
TEST 1

DIRECTIONS: Each question consists of a statement. You are to indicate whether the statement is TRUE (T) or FALSE (F). *PRINT THE LETTER OF THE CORRECT ANSWER IN THE SPACE AT THE RIGHT.*

1. The earliest existing astronomical records known at the time of writing Abell's text were of Chinese origin.   1.____

2. The clear weather in the region of the Sahara desert played a more important part in early astronomy than it does in modern astronomy.   2.____

3. The sun's principal apparent movement with respect to the stars is from west to east.   3.____

4. In winter the sun rises nearer to the north point of the horizon than in summer.   4.____

5. The apparent shape of the illuminated part of the moon as seen in the sky depends upon the difference in the direction from earth to sun and the direction from earth to moon.   5.____

6. At first quarter, the moon has the shape of a quarter circle.   6.____

7. Crescent, first quarter, full, gibbous, third quarter are words describing eclipses.   7.____

8. Phases of the moon are evidence of the spherical shape of the earth.   8.____

9. A computation of the size of the earth was a result of Eratosthenes's observation of the sun.   9.____

10. Planets generally move from east to west with respect to the stellar background.   10.____

11. A retrograding planet moves from east to west with respect to the stellar background.   11.____

12. The solar photosphere is hotter than the sunspot umbra.   12.____

13. If the largest possible fraction of the sky is to be observed, an observatory should be near the equator.   13.____

14. Copernicus's theories were based on his own astronomical observations.   14.____

15. "Superior" and "inferior" refer to distances of planets from the sun, with respect to the earth.   15.____

16. Inferior planets are most easily observed in conjunction with the sun.   16.____

17. Superior planets are most easily observed at opposition.   17.____

18. Pluto is called an inferior planet because it is one of the smallest planets.   18.____

19. The sideral period of revolution of a planet is the time required for the planet to move from conjunction with a star to conjunction with the same star as viewed from the sun.   19.____

20. All of the following planets, Mercury, Venus, Mars, Jupiter, Saturn, Uranus, Neptune and Pluto may appear in conjunction with the sun. 20._____

21. Full moon occurs at intervals determined by the moon's synodic period of revolution about the earth. 21._____

22. The synodic period of Mars is assumed to be exactly two years. The sidereal period then is two years. 22._____

23. The period of a planet whose distance from the sun is four astronomical units is eight years. Assume a circular orbit. 23._____

24. Telescopes were made by opticians for other uses before they were used in astronomy. 24._____

25. Kepler's GREATEST contributions to astronomy were based on Brahe's precision observations. 25._____

KEY (CORRECT ANSWERS)

1. T		11. T	
2. T		12. T	
3. T		13. T	
4. F		14. F	
5. T		15. T	
6. F		16. F	
7. F		17. T	
8. F		18. F	
9. T		19. T	
10. F		20. T	

21. T
22. T
23. T
24. T
25. T

TEST 2

DIRECTIONS: Each question consists of a statement. You are to indicate whether the statement is TRUE (T) or FALSE (F). *PRINT THE LETTER OF THE CORRECT ANSWER IN THE SPACE AT THE RIGHT.*

1. One of the modern forms of telescope was invented by Kepler. 1._____

2. Objects weigh less on the moon than on earth because the moon is less dense than earth. 2._____

3. When dropped from the same height, a cannon ball and a buckshot strike earth's surface at the same time. The explanation is the same gravitational acceleration of the buck-shot and the cannon ball. 3._____

4. Rotation of the earth causes points on the earth's equator to be more distant from the earth's center than a point at the north or south pole. 4._____

5. Aberration of starlight is a small apparent shift in the position of a star in a direction opposite to the direction of the earth's motion. 5._____

6. An eclipse CANNOT occur at winter solstice. 6._____

7. The albedo of the moon is its average temperature. 7._____

8. The path of totality of a solar eclipse is a narrow strip in the position of a star in a direction opposite to the direction of earth's motion. 8._____

9. An instantaneous photograph taken from an artificial satellite of a total solar eclipse on earth would show the zone of totality as a nearly circular spot. 9._____

10. During the total phase of a solar eclipse, sunspots can be observed within the zone of totality. 10._____

11. The sidereal day is always slightly longer than the solar day. 11._____

12. The sidereal day is defined as the interval between two successive transits of the vernal equinox. 12._____

13. Assume the plane of the moon's orbit to be in the plane of the ecliptic. During one sidereal month there would be two lunar eclipses. 13._____

14. Suppose the earth were completely covered with an ideal ocean. High tide at a given location would occur when the moon is on the horizon. 14._____

15. Observations of tides in solid earth show that the earth is as rigid as steel. 15._____

16. The earth's shape is MAINLY determined by its own gravitational attraction and its rotation. 16._____

17. The barycenter of the earth-moon system is halfway to the moon from the earth. 17._____

18. The length of a day is very gradually increasing. The increase is caused MAINLY by attractions of the other planets on the earth. 18._____

19. Measurements of the duration and the beginnings of the seasons led to the discovery of precession. 19.____

20. The rotation of a Foucault pendulum is a proof of the rotation of the earth. 20.____

21. As viewed from a crater near the moon's equator, the earth rises above the lunar horizon each earth month. 21.____

22. There may be as many as seven lunar and solar eclipses in one calendar year. 22.____

23. An observer mapping the moon from an observatory on earth would be able to see in several years' time more than half of the lunar surface. 23.____

24. Earth-shine is brightest on the moon when the earth is at quarter phase as seen from the moon. 24.____

25. If the moon revolved in its orbit in a direction opposite to its actual revolution, the synodic month would be longer than the sidereal month. 25.____

KEY (CORRECT ANSWERS)

1.	F	11.	F
2.	F	12.	T
3.	T	13.	F
4.	T	14.	F
5.	F	15.	T
6.	F	16.	T
7.	F	17.	F
8.	T	18.	F
9.	T	19.	T
10.	F	20.	T

21. F
22. T
23. T
24. F
25. F

TEST 3

DIRECTIONS: Each question consists of a statement. You are to indicate whether the statement is TRUE (T) or FALSE (F). *PRINT THE LETTER OF THE CORRECT ANSWER IN THE SPACE AT THE RIGHT.*

1. If one revolution of the earth around the sun took exactly 365 days, 3.000 hours, a leap year would be necessary each eight years.   1._____

2. A mass raised high above the earth's surface will weigh more than on earth.   2._____

3. Stellar parallax, retrograde motions, and aberration are effects of earth's revolution around the sun.   3._____

4. The latitude of the north pole is $0°$.   4._____

5. The ecliptic plane is the plane containing the earth's orbit.   5._____

6. The planets constitute APPROXIMATELY 10% of the entire mass of the solar system.   6._____

7. Sunspots are randomly distributed over the solar disk.   7._____

8. The retrograde rotation of Venus has been measured by radar signals from the earth that are reflected by fixed features on Venus's surface.   8._____

9. Some seasonal changes on Mars are marked by a shrinking of the south polar cap and a darkening of the maria.   9._____

10. The great red spot on Jupiter is a permanent feature of the planet which varies in size and color.   10._____

11. Saturn's rings are not solid sheets of material since stars are visible when occulted by the rings.   11._____

12. The inner planets, Mercury, Venus, Earth, Mars, are considerably less massive but denser than the outer planets.   12._____

13. Venus and Earth are nearly alike in mass and diameter but greatly different in rate of rotation.   13._____

14. Uranus and Neptune are nearly alike. They are similar to Jupiter and Saturn in mass.   14._____

15. The period of rotation of the planet Pluto has been obtained from observations of periodic variations of the brightness of the planet.   15._____

16. The LARGEST of the asteroids, Ceres, has a diameter of almost 500 miles.   16._____

17. The mass of an asteroid is estimated from its size and density.   17._____

18. Bode's law has a planetary position near the average of the positions of many asteroids.   18._____

19. The estimated combined masses of all the asteroids is about that of the moon.   19._____

20. The radio-reflecting layers of earth's atmosphere are concentrations of ionized atoms.   20._____

21. Many more impact craters would be present on the moon if it had a dense atmosphere. 21.____

22. Meteoritic impacts and some volcanic action seem to have formed the craters on the moon. 22.____

23. There is no direct evidence of collisions of meteors with the earth. 23.____

24. The sun is a huge "nuclear reactor" whose major energy source is the fusion of hydrogen to form helium. 24.____

25. "Canals" on Mars have not been observed from space vehicles. 25.____

KEY (CORRECT ANSWERS)

1. T
2. F
3. T
4. F
5. T

6. F
7. F
8. T
9. T
10. T

11. T
12. T
13. T
14. F
15. T

16. T
17. T
18. T
19. F
20. T

21. F
22. T
23. F
24. T
25. T

TEST 4

DIRECTIONS: Each question consists of a statement. You are to indicate whether the statement is TRUE (T) or FALSE (F). *PRINT THE LETTER OF THE CORRECT ANSWER IN THE SPACE AT THE RIGHT.*

1. Jupiter has a magnetic field and the associated "Van Allen" belts. 1._____
2. Pluto is at present believed to be comparable with Mars in diameter. 2._____
3. The radiant of a meteor swarm is a small area of the sky from which the meteors apparently diverge. 3._____
4. The ages of meteors are comparable with the age of the earth 4._____
5. Comets are sources of all meteorites. 5._____
6. If the moon is observed to rise at midnight, its phase is full. 6._____
7. The moon is the largest satellite in the solar system, in relation to its primary, earth. 7._____
8. The Jovian planets are composed of heavier elements than those that compose the earth. 8._____
9. The photosphere, chromosphere, ionosphere, and corona are all parts of the solar atmosphere. 9._____
10. Only the very largest meteors can reach the surface of the earth. 10._____
11. The earth reflects more sunlight than the moon. 11._____
12. A magnetic compass could be used on the moon to indicate directions from crater to crater. 12._____
13. The MOST abundant constituent of the earth's atmosphere is water vapor. 13._____
14. The core of the earth is the same density as the surface rocks. 14._____
15. The core of the earth is hotter than the surface rocks. 15._____
16. Slipping of rocks in fault zones causes earthquakes. 16._____
17. The mantle is the outermost layer of earth. 17._____
18. The age of the earth is believed to be about five billion years. 18._____
19. Lunar maria as viewed from the earth are smoother than other parts of the moon's surface. 19._____
20. Lunar maria are lighter in color than most other parts of the moon's surface. 20._____
21. Aurorae are caused by charged particles encountering the earth's atmosphere. 21._____
22. The lunar maria are generally younger than the lunar mountains. 22._____
23. Lunar rays are MOST easily seen during full moon. 23._____

24. The moon rotates once in the same time it takes to revolve once about the earth.   24.____

25. Mercury rotates on its axis with the same period as its period of revolution around the sun.   25.____

KEY (CORRECT ANSWERS)

1.	T	11.	T
2.	T	12.	F
3.	T	13.	F
4.	T	14.	F
5.	F	15.	T
6.	F	16.	T
7.	T	17.	F
8.	F	18.	T
9.	F	19.	T
10.	F	20.	F

21.	T
22.	T
23.	T
24.	T
25.	F

TEST 5

DIRECTIONS: Each question consists of a statement. You are to indicate whether the statement is TRUE (T) or FALSE *(F). PRINT THE LETTER OF THE CORRECT ANSWER IN THE SPACE AT THE RIGHT.*

1. The surface of Mercury is a good conductor of heat. 1.____
2. The mass and temperature of Mercury make it possible for this planet to hold an atmosphere. 2.____
3. Venus always appears as the morning star. 3.____
4. The surface of Venus is cooler than the surface of the earth. 4.____
5. Two satellites have been discovered revolving around Venus. 5.____
6. The MAJOR component of Venus's atmosphere is nitrogen. 6.____
7. The atmosphere of Venus is denser than earth's. 7.____
8. Artificial satellites near Venus have detected a magnetic field on the planet. 8.____
9. Mars has two satellites. 9.____
10. Mars is not an identical twin of the earth, it is smaller. 10.____
11. Comets always have tails. 11.____
12. The Martian atmosphere is denser than earth's atmosphere. 12.____
13. Mars's atmosphere is composed MAINLY of carbon dioxide. 13.____
14. Large yellow clouds on Mars are in composition much like clouds of water vapor on earth. 14.____
15. Jupiter has one dozen known satellites. 15.____
16. Jupiter's diameter is one hundred times earth's diameter. 16.____
17. Jupiter's mean density is less than earth's mean density. 17.____
18. The solar chromosphere is hotter than the corona. 18.____
19. The white bands on Jupiter are MOSTLY ammonia particles. 19.____
20. Radio observations show that Jupiter has a magnetic field. 20.____
21. If it were possible to find an ocean large enough to hold it, the planet Saturn would float. 21.____
22. Cassini's division is a gap between the two outermost rings of Saturn. 22.____
23. Saturn's atmosphere is very much like the atmosphere of Jupiter. 23.____
24. If Venus were at western elongation, it would be a "morning star." 24.____

25. One of the pieces of evidence that the relative positions of the continents may not have been the same in the past as they are at present is the existence of "magnetic anomalies" on the ocean floor.

25.____

KEY (CORRECT ANSWERS)

1.	F	11.	F
2.	F	12.	F
3.	F	13.	T
4.	F	14.	F
5.	F	15.	T
6.	F	16.	F
7.	T	17.	T
8.	F	18.	F
9.	T	19.	T
10.	T	20.	T

21. T
22. T
23. T
24. T
25. T

TEST 6

DIRECTIONS: Each question or incomplete statement is followed by several suggested answers or completions. Select the one that BEST answers the question or completes the statement. *PRINT THE LETTER OF THE CORRECT ANSWER IN THE SPACE AT THE RIGHT.*

1. Suppose you were an astronaut in orbit about the earth and you wish to overtake another spacecraft in the same orbit as you but some distance ahead. Assuming you are facing the direction you are traveling, your FIRST maneuver should be

    A. to fire rockets with their exhaust directed behind you
    B. to fire rockets with their exhaust directed in front of you
    C. to fire rockets with their exhaust directed below you
    D. none of the above

    1.____

2. What is the eccentricity of the orbit of a planet whose maximum and minimum distance from the sun are 1 AU and 1/2 AU?

    A. 1/3　　　B. 1/2　　　C. 2　　　D. 3

    2.____

3. The MOST important contribution of Copernicus to astronomy was to

    A. discover the relation between sidereal and synodic period
    B. eliminate epicycles
    C. put the sun, not the earth, as the central object in the solar system
    D. determine the relative distances of the planets

    3.____

4. Which of the following was NOT a reason advanced by Aristotle to prove that the earth was round?

    A. The earth's shadow on the moon during a lunar eclipse was always round
    B. If one went far enough in one direction, one came back to where he started
    C. Different stars were visible in Greece and in Egypt
    D. Elephants had been observed in both India and Morocco

    4.____

5. Hipparchus discovered the precession of the equinoxes by

    A. observing the motions of the stars
    B. comparing his coordinates for stars with those of earlier observers
    C. observing the motions of the sun
    D. adding epicycles to the model of Eudoxus

    5.____

6. An example of a superior planet is

    A. Mars　　　B. Venus　　　C. Earth　　　D. Moon

    6.____

7. Suppose an inferior planet has a synodic period of two years. What would its sidereal period be?

    A. 1/2 year　　　B. 2/3 year　　　C. 3/2 year　　　D. 2 years

    7.____

8. The effect of having uniform motion take place about a point that was displaced from the central object in the models of the "solar system" due to both Ptolemy and Copernicus was to approximate the motion summarized in Kepler's _____ law.

    A. first　　　B. second　　　C. third　　　D. none of the above

    8.____

9. As seen from the earth, direct motion of a planet is

   A. from west to east
   B. from east to west
   C. from north to south
   D. from south to north

10. Can the synodic period of a planet be less than 1 year?

    A. Yes
    B. No
    C. Sometimes
    D. It cannot be determined from the information given

11. What is the mass of a celestial object that has a satellite whose period of revolution is 10 times that of the moon around the earth and whose orbit is 100 times larger than that of the moon?

    A. 10^{-4} X mass of the earth
    B. 10^{-1} X mass of the earth
    C. 10 X mass of the earth
    D. 10^4 X mass of the earth

12. The evidence that the earth has a magnetic field is

    A. magnetic compasses work
    B. the Van Allen layers
    C. aurora
    D. all of these

13. The altitude of the north celestial pole is equal to

    A. the latitude of the observer
    B. 0°
    C. 90°
    D. 42°

14. A proof that the earth revolves around the sun is

    A. the change of direction of a Foucault pendulum
    B. the seasons
    C. the phases of Venus
    D. aberration of starlight

15. What is the azimuth of a star directly in the east and halfway from the horizon to the zenith?

    A. 45°
    B. 90°
    C. 270°
    D. 0°

16. What is the right ascension of the vernal equinox?

    A. 0^h
    B. 6^h
    C. 12^h
    D. 18^h

17. If the year were 720 days long, how far would the sun move each day with respect to the stars (as seen from the earth)?

    A. 1/2°
    B. 1°
    C. 2°
    D. None of these

18. In their studies of the heavens, the Greeks tried to

    A. predict the occurrence of "guest stars"
    B. make geometrical models of celestial objects
    C. predict the future positions of celestial objects by arithmetic techniques
    D. make geometrical models of the motions of celestial objects

19. You are on a strange planet. You note that the stars do not rise or set, but circle around parallel to the horizon. Then you travel over the surface of the planet in a straight line for 1,000 miles and find that at this new place the stars rise straight up from the horizon in the east and set straight down in the west. What is the circumference of the planet?

    A. 1,200/2π miles
    B. 2π X 1,000 miles
    C. 4,000 miles
    D. 4,000/2π miles

20. About what time of the day or night does the moon rise when it is at first quarter?

    A. Midnight
    B. Sunrise
    C. Noon
    D. Sunset

21. Suppose you were in a plane flying east and you cross the International Date Line. Before you cross it, the standard time is 9:45 Monday morning. What are the standard time and day 15 minutes later after you cross the line?

    A. 10 a.m. Sunday
    B. 11 a.m. Sunday
    C. 9 a.m. Tuesday
    D. 10 a.m. Tuesday

22. In what month would a star whose right ascension is 12^h be on the meridian at midnight local mean time?

    A. March
    B. September
    C. Neither of these
    D. Both A and B

23. The sidereal day is _____ the solar day.

    A. shorter than
    B. longer than
    C. equal to
    D. dependent upon

24. At the present time the MOST accurate way to measure the passage of time is

    A. with a quartz crystal clock
    B. by the rotation of the earth
    C. by occultations of stars by the moon
    D. with an atomic clock

25. Suppose a planet where 2 AU from the sun. It would receive _____ as much energy per unit area from the sun as does the earth.

    A. 1/4
    B. 1/2
    C. 2 times
    D. 4 times

KEY (CORRECT ANSWERS)

1.	B	11.	D
2.	A	12.	D
3.	C	13.	A
4.	B	14.	C
5.	B	15.	B
6.	A	16.	A
7.	B	17.	A
8.	B	18.	D
9.	B	19.	C
10.	A	20.	C

21. A
22. A
23. A
24. D
25. A

EXAMINATION SECTION
TEST 1

DIRECTIONS: Each question or incomplete statement is followed by several suggested answers or completions. Select the one that BEST answers the question or completes the statement. *PRINT THE LETTER OF THE CORRECT ANSWER IN THE SPACE AT THE RIGHT.*

1. We see one-half of the lighted portion of the moon at the
   - A. first quarter
   - B. full moon
   - C. new crescent
   - D. new moon

2. A planet whose orbit is between the sun and the orbit of the earth is
   - A. Jupiter
   - B. Mars
   - C. Pluto
   - D. Venus

3. The changing position of the stars during the night is MAINLY the result of the
   - A. *inclination* of the earth's axis
   - B. *rotation* of the earth
   - C. *rotation* of the stars
   - D. *revolution* of the earth

4. The gravitational force of the moon is exerted
   - A. only upon the side of the earth nearest the moon
   - B. only upon the point on the earth nearest the moon
   - C. upon the center of the earth only
   - D. upon the entire earth

5. The work done by tides is gradually slowing down the earth's period of rotation. It is, therefore, reasonable to predict that millions of years from now,
   - A. the earth will be farther away from the moon than now
   - B. the frequency of tides will be greater than now
   - C. days will be shorter than they are now
   - D. phases of the moon will change more rapidly than now

6. The earth's gravitational attraction is GREATEST at
   - A. the North Pole
   - B. the Equator
   - C. a point on the earth's surface directly under the moon
   - D. a point on the earth's surface exactly opposite the moon

7. The twinkling of a star is caused by
   - A. the star itself
   - B. interplanetary dust
   - C. defects in the structure of the human eye
   - D. turbulence within the atmosphere

8. The small dipper seems to turn about the North Star once each day because

A. all stars move in great circles on the celestial sphere
B. the earth turns on its axis
C. the North Star is the last star in the handle of the dipper
D. the planets revolve around the sun

9. The stars that comprise the Big Dipper are of which one of the following magnitudes?

    A. +1   B. +2   C. +3   D. +4

10. The distance of any remote group of stars can be determined if the group contains which one of the following?

    A. Double stars
    B. Dwarf stars
    C. Super giant stars
    D. Cepheid variable stars

11. Among the following, the expression that BEST describes the typical star in old age is

    A. blue giant
    B. blue-white intermediary
    C. yellow giant
    D. red dwarf

12. According to Hubble, the galaxies are BEST classified into which one of the following sets of categories?

    A. Elliptical and spherical
    B. Elliptical and spiral
    C. Spherical and spiral
    D. Elliptical, spherical, and spiral

13. Any given point on the moon receives continuous light for a number of days CLOSEST to which one of the following?

    A. 7   B. 10   C. 14   D. 29

14. If the first quarter moon rises at noon, the last quarter moon will rise at a time CLOSEST to which one of the following?

    A. Midnight   B. 3 A.M.   C. 3 P.M.   D. 6 P.M.

15. The concept that distant stars are receding from the earth at great velocity is implied from observation of the

    A. Cepheid variables
    B. parallax
    C. red giants changing toward white
    D. spectroscopic shift to the red

16. On the eastern coast, the altitude of the North Star is CLOSEST to which one of the following?

    A. 39°   B. 42°   C. 45°   D. $47\frac{1}{2}$°

17. Which one of the following constellations seems to dip below the horizon in New York City?

    A. Cassiopeia   B. Cepheus   C. Orion   D. Ursa Major

18. When Venus is in line with the earth and the sun, on the side of the sun nearest the earth, it is

    A. at inferior conjunction
    B. at superior conjunction
    C. in opposition
    D. at an elongation of 180°

19. Studies of Cepheid variable stars have been of MOST value in revealing which one of the following?

    A. Nature of atomic fusion
    B. Magnitude of stars
    C. Distance of galaxies
    D. Size of galaxies

20. Which one of the following statements is TRUE regarding the tide-producing force of the moon? It varies

    A. *directly* with the distance
    B. *directly* with the square of the distance
    C. *inversely* with the square of the distance
    D. *inversely* with the cube of the distance

21. Which one of the following constellations is CLOSEST to the celestial north pole?

    A. Ursa Minor   B. Ursa Major   C. Cepheus   D. Draco

22. Which one of the following discovered the harmonic law relating distance of a planet to its time of revolution?

    A. Tycho Brahe   B. Kepler   C. Galileo   D. Newton

23. As nearly as can be estimated, the center line of the Milky Way is the

    A. celestial equator
    B. plane of the ecliptic
    C. celestial meridian
    D. galactic equator

24. A planet which is NEVER visible at night is

    A. Mars   B. Neptune   C. Mercury   D. Saturn

25. The planetoids are located between

    A. Earth and Mars
    B. Mars and Venus
    C. Mars and Jupiter
    D. Jupiter and Saturn

4 (#1)

KEY (CORRECT ANSWERS)

1.	A	11.	D
2.	D	12.	B
3.	B	13.	C
4.	D	14.	A
5.	A	15.	D
6.	A	16.	B
7.	D	17.	C
8.	B	18.	A
9.	B	19.	C
10.	D	20.	D

21. A
22. B
23. D
24. C
25. C

TEST 2

DIRECTIONS: Each question or incomplete statement is followed by several suggested answers or completions. Select the one that BEST answers the question or completes the statement. *PRINT THE LETTER OF THE CORRECT ANSWER IN THE SPACE AT THE RIGHT.*

1. At which one of these phases does the moon rise APPROXIMATELY at midnight and set APPROXIMATELY at noon?   1.____

    A. New
    B. Full
    C. First quarter
    D. Last quarter

2. The planetoids are located with GREATEST frequency between   2.____

    A. Earth and Mars
    B. Jupiter and Saturn
    C. Mars and Venus
    D. Mars and Jupiter

3. When the moon is between the earth and the sun and in line with them, the tidal range on the earth at any one place is   3.____

    A. average
    B. less than average
    C. more than average
    D. at maximum

4. All stars visible to the naked eye belong to   4.____

    A. the Milky Way galaxy
    B. a number of galaxies
    C. the solar system
    D. the Milky Way galaxy and several spiral nebulae

5. Of the following planets, the one that has its orbital plane MOST inclined to the ecliptic is   5.____

    A. Mercury   B. Earth   C. Saturn   D. Pluto

6. Among the characteristics listed, the one in which stars differ LEAST is   6.____

    A. diameter
    B. mass
    C. density
    D. distance from the earth

7. The NEAREST star to the earth is   7.____

    A. the sun
    B. the moon
    C. Polaris
    D. Alpha Centauri

8. Among the following, the statement about TIROS that is NOT true is that   8.____

    A. the name is an acronym for Television and Infra-Red Observation Satellite
    B. it is used principally for weather observation
    C. it is powered by nuclear batteries
    D. it is unmanned

9. Primary cosmic rays are believed to consist MOSTLY of which one of the following?   9.____

    A. Photons   B. Protons   C. Mesons   D. Neutrons

10. Among the following, the planet that has the MOST eccentric orbit is   10.____

    A. Mercury   B. Earth   C. Saturn   D. Pluto

77

11. Of the following, the color exhibited by the HOTTEST star is

    A. red   B. yellow   C. blue-white   D. orange

12. Spring tides are MOST likely to occur at the phase of the moon called

    A. first quarter   B. full moon
    C. gibbous   D. crescent

13. If the moon were to stop rotating, we would

    A. see both sides of it
    B. have higher tides
    C. have full moon continuously
    D. have half moon continuously

14. The North Star is found in which one of the following constellations?

    A. The Little Dipper   B. The Big Dipper
    C. Orion   D. Arcturus

15. At the autumnal equinox, the vertical rays of the sun at noon are over the

    A. Tropic of Cancer   B. Tropic of Capricorn
    C. Arctic Circle   D. Equator

16. The planet whose diameter is CLOSEST in size to that of the earth is

    A. Mercury   B. Venus   C. Mars   D. Neptune

17. The time required for the sun to pass a given meridian twice in succession is called a _____ day.

    A. mean solar   B. sidereal   C. solar   D. civil

18. The altitude of the North Star is CLOSEST to 65° at which one of the following locations?

    A. Arctic Circle   B. City of New York
    C. North Pole   D. Tropic of Cancer

19. If a full moon occurs on June 1st, the next new moon phase will take place at a time CLOSEST to which one of the following?

    A. June 8   B. June 15   C. June 22   D. June 29

20. Circular star trails are evidence that the

    A. earth is revolving   B. stars are revolving
    C. stars are rotating   D. earth is rotating

21. Of the following heavenly bodies, the one which has come CLOSEST to the earth in historic times is a

    A. moon   B. meteor   C. planet   D. comet

22. The Milky Way is classified as which one of the following?

    A. Star   B. Solar system   C. Galaxy   D. Constellation

23. Of the following, the BEST description of the earth's orbit is that it is

    A. circular
    B. highly elliptical
    C. slightly elliptical
    D. three-dimensional

24. The moon's orbit around the earth is BEST described as a(n)

    A. ellipse
    B. straight line
    C. hyperbola
    D. circle

25. When the moon rises approximately at noon and sets at about midnight, its phase is

    A. new moon
    B. last quarter
    C. first quarter
    D. full moon

KEY (CORRECT ANSWERS)

1.	D	11.	C
2.	D	12.	B
3.	D	13.	A
4.	A	14.	A
5.	D	15.	D
6.	B	16.	B
7.	A	17.	C
8.	C	18.	A
9.	B	19.	B
10.	D	20.	D

21. B
22. C
23. C
24. A
25. C

TEST 3

DIRECTIONS: Each question or incomplete statement is followed by several suggested answers or completions. Select the one that BEST answers the question or completes the statement. *PRINT THE LETTER OF THE CORRECT ANSWER IN THE SPACE AT THE RIGHT.*

1. A planet which is NOT visible to the naked eye is 1.____

   A. Saturn   B. Neptune   C. Mars   D. Venus

2. All of the stars visible to the naked eye in our sky are members of 2.____

   A. the solar system   B. a group of galaxies
   C. the Milky Way galaxy   D. the Andromeda galaxy

3. Spring tides occur when 3.____

   A. the gravitational forces of the sun and moon affect the earth in the same direction
   B. the sun's gravitational force acts at right angles to that of the moon
   C. the moon is in the new crescent phase
   D. none of the above

4. Of the following stars, the one FARTHEST from the earth is 4.____

   A. Sirius   B. Polaris   C. Proxima Centauri   D. Betelgeuse

5. The FAINTEST star that the unaided eye can see is classified as a star of the _____ magnitude. 5.____

   A. first   B. second   C. third   D. sixth

6. The GREATEST source of radio energy yet discovered by radio astronomy lies in the constellation 6.____

   A. Orion   B. Ursa Major   C. Cyngus   D. Canis Major

7. The new-moon phase occurs when the moon is at 7.____

   A. conjunction   B. opposition
   C. elongation   D. quadrature

8. The BRIGHTEST of all the fixed stars observed from earth is 8.____

   A. Betelgeuse   B. Formalhaut   C. Sirius   D. Vega

9. An eclipse of the moon occurs when the 9.____

   A. moon passes between the earth and the sun
   B. sun passes between the earth and the moon
   C. earth passes between the sun and the moon
   D. new moon phase occurs

10. A reading taken in New York City would indicate that the magnetic north pole is located _____ the geographic north pole. 10.____

    A. at   B. east of   C. due south of   D. west of

11. The earth is classified as a 11.____

    A. star B. comet C. satellite D. planet

12. One effect among the following of the earth's rotation on its axis is the 12.____

    A. daily westward shift of stars
    B. variation in the seasons
    C. moon's phases
    D. formation of circular star trails in the polar region

13. The planet whose solid surface can be observed is 13.____

    A. Venus B. Mars C. Saturn D. Jupiter

14. The phase of the moon at which it rises CLOSEST to noontime is 14.____

    A. new moon   B. full moon
    C. first quarter   D. last quarter

15. The surface temperature of a blue-white star is CLOSEST, in degrees F, to 15.____

    A. 11,000 B. 20,000 C. 28,000 D. 36,000

16. The MAXIMUM possible duration of a total lunar eclipse is CLOSEST to 16.____

    A. 15 minutes B. 30 minutes C. 1 hour D. 2 hours

17. A satellite with an average distance of 300 miles above the earth's surface would revolve around the earth in a period CLOSEST to 17.____

    A. 50 minutes B. 90 minutes C. 10 hours D. 24 hours

18. Of the following, the one generally credited with sponsoring the heliocentric theory of the solar system is 18.____

    A. Aristotle   B. Copernicus
    C. Hippocrates D. Ptolemy

19. Karl Jansky was the discoverer of 19.____

    A. a naked-eye comet in 1958
    B. a new moon of Jupiter
    C. radio waves from outer space
    D. the F layer of the ionosphere

20. According to modern concepts of the life history of a star, a dwarf star represents the stage of star 20.____

    A. birth B. youth C. maturity D. old age

21. If Star A is a 5th magnitude star and Star B is a 2nd magnitude star, then the ratio of the brightness of B to that of A is CLOSEST to 21.____

    A. 2.5 B. 3.0 C. 9.0 D. 15.0

22. Which one of the following is a first magnitude star in the constellation Orion?

    A. Altair   B. Aldebaran   C. Betelgeuse   D. Sirius

23. Earthshine is MOST prominent at the phase of the moon called

    A. new crescent
    C. full moon
    B. first quarter
    D. old gibbous

24. The moon's speed of revolution is

    A. greatest at apogee
    B. greatest at perigee
    C. greatest at new moon phase
    D. uniform throughout its orbit

25. Quantitative analysis of the stars through spectrographic study indicates that the stars consist of APPROXIMATELY

    A. 50% uranium
    B. 75% hydrogen
    C. 20% thorium
    D. the same percentage composition of elements as the earth

---

KEY (CORRECT ANSWERS)

1. B
2. C
3. A
4. D
5. D

6. C
7. A
8. C
9. C
10. D

11. D
12. D
13. B
14. C
15. C

16. D
17. B
18. B
19. C
20. D

21. D
22. C
23. A
24. B
25. B

TEST 4

DIRECTIONS: Each question or incomplete statement is followed by several suggested answers or completions. Select the one that BEST answers the question or completes the statement. *PRINT THE LETTER OF THE CORRECT ANSWER IN THE SPACE AT THE RIGHT.*

1. The manner of occultation of a planet by the moon shows that the moon demonstrates which one of the following characteristics?

    A. Lacks an atmosphere
    B. Moves faster than the planet in miles per hour
    C. Rotates on its axis
    D. Frequently changes its axis of rotation

2. The moon moves MOST rapidly in its orbit at

    A. apogee   B. full moon   C. new moon   D. perigee

3. Mercury has a low albedo because of its

    A. high temperature   B. small size
    C. small mass   D. lack of atmosphere

4. Astronomers have found that, as viewed from the earth,

    A. all galaxies are receding at the same speed
    B. some galaxies are approaching the earth
    C. the more distant the galaxy, the greater its speed of recession
    D. the more distant the galaxy, the less its speed of recession

5. In astronomy, the measure which corresponds to longitude is called

    A. declination   B. right ascension
    C. left ascension   D. zenith variation

6. The theory of the expanding universe of the stars is based largely on the evidence that analysis of light coming from the distant stars shows

    A. a decrease in wave-length
    B. a shift toward the violet end of the spectrum
    C. no shift in Fraunhofer lines
    D. a shift toward the longer wave-lengths

7. Telstar went into orbit with a speed of approximately 18,000 miles per hour at perigee, which is about 600 miles. If apogee is approximately 3500 miles, its speed at apogee should be, in miles per hour, CLOSEST to which one of the following?

    A. 6,000   B. 11,000   C. 16,000   D. 18,000

8. The study of tidal effects and careful measurement have led to which one of the following conclusions?

    A. The period of the earth's rotation is gradually decreasing.
    B. Tidal forces are greater on earth than they are on the moon.
    C. The moon is slowly spiraling outward from the earth.
    D. The moon's period of rotation is decreasing.

9. The ecliptic is ALWAYS inclined 23.5° to the

   A. celestial equator
   B. horizon
   C. Tropic of Cancer
   D. diurnal circle

10. As a planet revolves about the sun, its speed

    A. is constant
    B. increases as it approaches the sun
    C. decreases as it gets closer to the sun
    D. varies so that all planets complete one revolution in 365 days

11. The ratio of the brightness of a star of magnitude 3 to that of a star of magnitude 4 is

    A. 2:5   B. 3:4   C. 4:3   D. 5:2

12. All of the following statements regarding a solar eclipse are true EXCEPT that

    A. it can occur only once in any calendar year
    B. it can occur only at new moon phase
    C. at any one point on the earth, the maximum duration of a total eclipse is about 7 minutes
    D. the maximum width of the moon's umbra on the earth is approximately 167 miles

13. The ratio of the distance from the sun of a theoretical solar system planet with a period of revolution of eight earth years to the earth's distance from the sun is CLOSEST to which one of the following?

    A. 2:1   B. $2\sqrt{2}:1$ C. 4:1   D. 8:1

14. As their distance from the earth changes, planets

    A. change in brightness and apparent size
    B. change in brightness but not in apparent size
    C. change in apparent size but not in brightness
    D. do not change in brightness or apparent size

15. Which one of the following is known for having obtained evidence of the rotation of the earth?

    A. Archimedes   B. Foucault   C. Maury   D. Wright

16. The gravitational force between two bodies in space varies

    A. *directly* with the distance between them
    B. *inversely* with the distance between them
    C. *inversely* with the square of the distance between them
    D. *directly* with the square of the distance between them

17. If the inclination of the earth's axis were 45°, the summers in New York City would be

    A. cooler   B. warmer   C. shorter   D. longer

18. Of the following, the one MOST closely associated with the production of solar energy is

    A. burning of hydrogen gas
    B. fusion of hydrogen nuclei
    C. fission of U^{235} nuclei
    D. fission of helium nuclei

19. During which phase of the moon is an eclipse of the sun MOST likely to occur?

    A. New   B. Full   C. Quarter   D. Gibbous

20. Which one of the following scientists discovered laws governing the motion of planets?

    A. Roentgen   B. Wöhler   C. Foucault   D. Kepler

21. Circular star trails seen in photographs are an effect of

    A. the revolution of the earth about the sun
    B. cosmic radiation
    C. the rotation of the earth
    D. an expanding universe

22. Of the following, the constellation NOT visible in the Northern Hemisphere in the winter sky is

    A. Lyra   B. Cassiopeia   C. Ursa Major   D. Ursa Minor

23. The rays of the sun are vertical over the Tropic of Capricorn at a time CLOSEST to which one of the following dates?

    A. March 21   B. June 21   C. September 21   D. December 21

24. Moonrise occurs CLOSEST to solar noon at the phase of the moon known as

    A. first quarter   B. full moon
    C. third quarter   D. new moon

25. The bright star Capella is in the constellation

    A. Auriga   B. Bootes   C. Lyra   D. Scorpius

KEY (CORRECT ANSWERS)

1.	A	11.	A
2.	D	12.	A
3.	D	13.	C
4.	C	14.	A
5.	B	15.	B
6.	D	16.	C
7.	B	17.	B
8.	C	18.	B
9.	A	19.	A
10.	B	20.	D

21. C
22. A
23. D
24. A
25. A

EXAMINATION SECTION
TEST 1

DIRECTIONS: Each question or incomplete statement is followed by several suggested answers or completions. Select the one that BEST answers the question or completes the statement. *PRINT THE LETTER OF THE CORRECT ANSWER IN THE SPACE AT THE RIGHT.*

1. The synodical month is

    A. about two days longer than the sidereal month
    B. about three days shorter than the sidereal month
    C. 31 days long on the average
    D. the time required for the moon to revolve 360°

2. Betelgeuse and Rigel are navigational stars in the constellation

    A. Cassiopeia   B. Lyra   C. Orion   D. Ursa Major

3. Which one of the following statements about the planet Jupiter is NOT true?

    A. All of its moons revolve from west to east.
    B. Its rotation period is shorter than any other planet.
    C. It has more natural moons than any other planet.
    D. Some of Jupiter's moons are larger than the planet Mercury.

4. The principal reason that an eclipse of the moon does NOT occur every full moon is that the

    A. difference between perigee and apogee is too large
    B. refraction of sunlight interferes
    C. earth's shadow barely reaches the moon
    D. moon's orbit is inclined to the plane of the earth's orbit

5. The ratio of the diameter of the sun to that of Jupiter is CLOSEST to which one of the following?

    A. 5:1   B. 10:1   C. 25:1   D. 100:1

6. Of the following gases, the one MOST prominent in the atmosphere of Jupiter is

    A. acetylene   B. methane
    C. nitric oxide   D. sulfur dioxide

7. At the level of tropopause, the MOST abundant gas in the atmosphere is

    A. hydrogen   B. helium   C. oxygen   D. nitrogen

8. The planet with the GREATEST orbital speed is

    A. Earth   B. Mercury   C. Neptune   D. Pluto

9. Of the following, the FIRST scientist to use the astronomical telescope was

    A. Galileo   B. Kepler   C. Leeuwenhoek   D. Tycho Brahe

10. In an annular eclipse of the sun,

    A. both the umbra and penumbra of the moon touch the earth
    B. the moon's umbra touches the earth, but the penumbra does not
    C. the moon's penumbra touches the earth, but the umbra does not
    D. neither the umbra nor the penumbra of the moon touches the earth

11. Of the following, the one which is an example of a diffuse nebula is the

    A. Great Cluster in Hercules
    B. Great Nebula in Orion
    C. Great Spiral in Andromeda
    D. Milky Way

12. The atmosphere of which one of the following planets is rich in methane and ammonia?

    A. Venus   B. Mercury   C. Jupiter   D. Mars

13. The ratio of the volume of the earth to that of the moon is CLOSEST to which one of the following?

    A. 4:1   B. 8:1   C. 32:1   D. 64:1

14. Which one of the following statements is TRUE of the stars of the same spectral class? They

    A. are all equidistant from the sun
    B. are all blue-white stars
    C. are all Cepheid variables
    D. all have approximately the same surface temperature

15. Of the following, the diameter of our galaxy in light-years is CLOSEST to

    A. 1,000   B. 10,000   C. 100,000   D. 1,000,000

16. According to modern astronomical theory, the average lifetime for a star is CLOSEST, in years, to which one of the following?

    A. 10 million   B. 100 million   C. 1 billion   D. 10 billion

17. Of the following, the layer of the sun whose thickness is SMALLEST is the

    A. chromosphere
    B. corona
    C. photosphere
    D. reversing layer

18. Rigel is a navigational star in which one of the following constellations?

    A. Orion   B. Canis Major   C. Cassiopeia   D. Ursa Major

19. Which one of the following constellations is MOST commonly used as an aid in finding the North Star?

    A. Orion   B. Pleiades   C. Taurus   D. Ursa Major

20. Which one of the following planets is 1.52 astronomical units from the sun?

    A. Saturn   B. Mars   C. Venus   D. Mercury

21. Cepheid variable stars go through a light cycle which, at its maximum, may be as long as   21.____

    A. 1 hour
    B. 1 day
    C. several weeks
    D. several years

22. Astronomers use the term *magnitude* to denote   22.____

    A. size of stars
    B. apparent brightness
    C. telescope range
    D. telescope magnification ratio

23. When the earth is farthest from the sun, the season in the earth's Southern Hemisphere is   23.____

    A. spring   B. summer   C. fall   D. winter

24. The interval of 18 years, 11 1/3 days after which a cycle of solar and lunar eclipses is repeated, is known as the   24.____

    A. ecliptic limit
    B. eclipse season
    C. saros
    D. albedo

25. The average length of the synodic month is CLOSEST to which one of the following? _____ days.   25.____

    A. 27.5   B. 29.5   C. 31.5   D. 33.5

KEY (CORRECT ANSWERS)

1. A
2. C
3. A
4. D
5. B
6. B
7. D
8. B
9. A
10. C
11. B
12. C
13. D
14. D
15. C
16. D
17. C
18. A
19. D
20. B
21. C
22. B
23. D
24. C
25. B

TEST 2

DIRECTIONS: Each question or incomplete statement is followed by several suggested answers or completions. Select the one that BEST answers the question or completes the statement. *PRINT THE LETTER OF THE CORRECT ANSWER IN THE SPACE AT THE RIGHT.*

1. The planet in our solar system NEAREST in size to the earth is   1.____
   A. Mars   B. Mercury   C. Neptune   D. Venus

2. Of the following, a star of the SECOND apparent visual magnitude is the star   2.____
   A. Arcturus   B. Polaris   C. Procyon   D. Rigel

3. The famous Horsehead Nebula in Orion is a   3.____
   A. cluster of stars   B. dark nebula
   C. galaxy   D. Magellanic Cloud

4. The planet in our solar system with the MOST eccentric orbit is   4.____
   A. Jupiter   B. Mercury   C. Pluto   D. Uranus

5. The great telescope at Jodrell Bank, England, is a   5.____
   A. radiotelescope   B. prism
   C. refractor   D. Schmidt telescope

6. Astronomers use spectroscopes to   6.____
   A. measure the distance to stars
   B. determine the mass of stars
   C. determine the size of stars
   D. analyze the light from stars

7. The planet with the LARGEST number of moons is   7.____
   A. Mars   B. Jupiter   C. Saturn   D. Uranus

8. The Milky Way is a   8.____
   A. galaxy   B. constellation
   C. spiral nebula   D. solar system

9. Of the following, the planet that shows phases when viewed through the telescope is   9.____
   A. Mars   B. Venus   C. Saturn   D. Jupiter

10. Of the following, the star of the second apparent magnitude is   10.____
    A. Altair   B. Aldebaran   C. Polaris   D. Rigel

11. Of the following, a star in the constellation Lyra is   11.____
    A. Antares   B. Capella   C. Sirius   D. Vega

12. Our sun is classed as a(n) _____ star.

    A. average-size B. dwarf
    C. giant D. super-giant

13. Man-made satellites travelling about the earth in elliptical orbits are CLOSEST to the earth at their

    A. nadir B. perigee C. apogee D. zenith

14. A planet which can NEVER be seen from the earth at midnight is

    A. Mars B. Venus C. Jupiter D. Saturn

15. The orbits of the comets are USUALLY

    A. circles B. ellipses C. parabolas D. hyperbolas

16. The SECOND largest planet in our solar system is

    A. Jupiter B. Neptune C. Uranus D. Saturn

17. A celestial object which is NOT a part of our galaxy is the

    A. Great Spiral Nebula in Andromeda
    B. Great Nebula in Orion
    C. Great Cluster in Hercules
    D. Omega Centauri

18. A star whose apparent visual magnitude is expressed as a negative number is

    A. Algol B. Betelgeuse C. Spica D. Sirius

19. The earth revolves around the sun at a speed, in miles per hour, of about

    A. 25,000 B. 66,000 C. 93,000 D. 186,000

20. The planet with the SHORTEST period of rotation is

    A. Earth B. Mars C. Mercury D. Jupiter

21. When Mercury and Venus are morning stars,

    A. both are seen near the eastern horizon
    B. both are seen near the western horizon
    C. Mercury is in the east, Venus in the west
    D. Mercury is in the west, Venus in the east

22. The dark side of the moon cannot be observed from the earth because the moon

    A. revolves around the earth, but does not rotate on its axis
    B. rotates about its axis, but does not revolve around the earth
    C. has the same period of rotation as its period of revolution
    D. has a period of rotation of 24 hours and a period of revolution of 30 days

23. The SMALLEST of the planets in the solar system is

    A. Mars B. Uranus C. Pluto D. Mercury

24. An astronomical feature which lies beyond the limits of the Milky Way is   24._____
    A. the Pleiades cluster
    B. the Perseids
    C. Halley's Comet
    D. the Great Nebula in Andromeda

25. The famous Horsehead Nebula is in the constellation   25._____
    A. Canis Major   B. Orion   C. Taurus   D. Sagittarius

KEY (CORRECT ANSWERS)

1. D
2. B
3. B
4. C
5. A

6. D
7. B
8. A
9. B
10. C

11. D
12. A
13. B
14. B
15. B

16. D
17. A
18. D
19. B
20. D

21. A
22. C
23. D
24. D
25. B

TEST 3

DIRECTIONS: Each question or incomplete statement is followed by several suggested answers or completions. Select the one that BEST answers the question or completes the statement. *PRINT THE LETTER OF THE CORRECT ANSWER IN THE SPACE AT THE RIGHT.*

1. The phase of the moon which is viewed when the moon sets shortly after the sun is called the

    A. new crescent
    B. first quarter
    C. new gibbous
    D. last quarter

    1._____

2. The Perseids are a

    A. meteor swarm
    B. group of planetoids
    C. group of sunspots
    D. star cluster in the constellation Perseus

    2._____

3. Auroras or northern lights are believed to be caused by

    A. reflection of sunlight from the polar icecap
    B. streams of electrically-charged particles deflected and concentrated by the earth's magnetic field
    C. diffraction of sunlight by ice crystals in the upper atmosphere
    D. disintegration of radioactive elements in the earth's atmosphere

    3._____

4. Neap tides occur when there is a

    A. full moon
    B. new moon
    C. lunar eclipse
    D. moon at first quarter phase

    4._____

5. When an artificial satellite orbits the earth, its position CLOSEST to the earth is known as

    A. perigee   B. aphelion   C. apogee   D. perihelion

    5._____

6. Of the following, the statement which is NOT true is that the sun

    A. is a star
    B. is a stationary body
    C. varies in its distance from the earth
    D. rotates on its axis

    6._____

7. The earth is FARTHEST from the sun in

    A. January   B. March   C. July   D. October

    7._____

8. The constellation that can be seen at any time of the year in New York is

    A. Cassiopeia   B. Orion   C. Andromeda   D. Leo

    8._____

9. A star in the constellation Orion is

   A. Antares   B. Arcturus   C. Capella   D. Rigel

10. Two stars differ in apparent brightness by exactly one magnitude. The ratio of their apparent brightness is, therefore,

    A. 1:1   B. 1:2.5   C. 1:5.0   D. 1:10

11. In light-gathering power, a 200" reflecting telescope is GREATER than a 100" reflecting telescope by a ratio of

    A. 2:1   B. 4:1   C. 16:1   D. 100:1

12. A wide-angle type of reflecting telescope especially adapted to photographing large areas of the heavens is known as the

    A. Balmer   B. Cassegrainian
    C. Newtonian   D. Schmidt

13. The ratio of the light reflected by a planet to that received on its whole illuminated hemisphere is called its

    A. albedo   B. insolation
    C. luminosity   D. noctilucence

14. The shift of the red lines in the spectrum of light reaching us from distant galaxies (Doppler effect) makes it possible to determine their

    A. temperatures
    B. velocities and directions of movement
    C. sizes and shapes
    D. chemical compositions

15. The planet in our solar system which has the MOST eccentric orbit around the sun is

    A. Uranus   B. Pluto   C. Neptune   D. Saturn

16. To an observer on Earth, the BRIGHTEST planet is

    A. Jupiter   B. Saturn   C. Mars   D. Venus

17. The Russian Lunik revolved around the

    A. sun outside the earth's orbit
    B. sun inside the earth's orbit
    C. moon
    D. earth

18. The Northern Cross lies in the constellation

    A. Cygnus   B. Bootes   C. Lyra   D. Pegasus

19. A galaxy visible to the unaided eye lies in the constellation

    A. Andromeda   B. Ursa Minor   C. Auriga   D. Canis Major

20. Spring tides occur at

   A. full moon only
   B. new moon only
   C. both full and new moon
   D. first and last quarter phases

21. An annular eclipse of the sun takes place at the phase of the moon called

   A. new moon
   B. new gibbous
   C. new crescent
   D. full moon

22. At perigee, our moon's distance, expressed in miles, from the earth is about

   A. 205,000   B. 220,000   C. 235,000   D. 245,000

23. Moore and Ross recently ascended to a height of 80,000 ft. and discovered

   A. cosmic ray bombardment from space
   B. the nature of the rings of Saturn
   C. water vapor in the atmosphere of Venus
   D. new values for the space unit Mach

24. All stars visible to the naked eye belong to

   A. the solar system
   B. a number of galaxies
   C. the Milky Way galaxy
   D. the Milky Way galaxy and several spiral nebulae

25. The BRIGHTEST star visible in the nightime sky in New York City is

   A. Betelgeuse   B. Orion   C. Polaris   D. Sirius

KEY (CORRECT ANSWERS)

1. A
2. A
3. B
4. D
5. A

6. B
7. C
8. A
9. D
10. B

11. B
12. D
13. A
14. B
15. B

16. D
17. A
18. A
19. A
20. C

21. A
22. B
23. C
24. C
25. D

BASIC FUNDAMENTALS OF ASTRONOMY

CONTENTS

	Page
Chapter 1 - The Universe	1
Chapter 2 - Stars and Galaxies	6
Chapter 3 - The Sun	11
Chapter 4 - The Solar System	16
Chapter 5 - The Moon	21
Chapter 6 - The Earth	26

BASIC FUNDAMENTALS OF ASTRONOMY

CHAPTER 1

THE UNIVERSE

Astronomers, who study the stars, tell us that we live in a universe filled with millions and millions of stars like our sun. The universe is so large that it takes light thousands of millions of years to move the distances we can see in our telescopes. How did the astronomers learn about the stars and the great distances in space? This is the question we shall try to answer in this chapter.

Radiation

Every star, like our sun, is extremely hot inside. A star is a nuclear furnace, busy changing the element hydrogen into the element helium. This process produces vast amounts of energy. If you go to a beach in the summertime and your skin tans, you have used some of that energy. Every morsel of food you eat has been grown by the sun's energy. How does this energy reach the earth? It comes in the same way a radio broadcast reaches your radio. It is sent through space as radiation.

A radio station broadcasts on one frequency. We must tune to that frequency to hear the station. The stars broadcast their radiation on many frequencies. One of these frequencies - called the ultraviolet range - is tuned in by your skin. The energy on this frequency is used to tan the skin. Some of the frequencies coming from the stars can be seen by human eyes. We call these frequencies *light*. Others are like radio waves - they cannot be seen. The whole universe is filled with these radiations coming from the stars.

Light

On most clear nights we can see the moon in the sky. But the moon does not shine or radiate. It is a dead body. We can see the moon only because light from the sun is reflected from it to earth. In fact, the only reason we can see anything at all is that light reflects into our eyes from different objects in different ways. We have learned how to interpret these reflections. We say that we see things. Actually, we see the light that reflects off things and reaches our eyes. When there is no light, we cannot see things at all. But they are still there. That is why we bump into solid objects when we are walking in the dark.

Because sight is very important to us and we see only if there is light, scientists have studied it very carefully. They have learned and put to use a number of facts about light. Here are five of the most important characteristics of light that scientists use.

First, *light moves at a constant speed*. When we snap on a light switch, the light floods the room instantly. Or so it seems to us because it moves so fast. Scientists have been able to measure the speed of light. They find that it moves at a speed of about 186,000 miles per second. Radio waves and electricity travel at this same rate of speed. In fact, scientists believe that nothing else in the universe travels faster than light. Because light moves at a steady speed, it can be used for measuring. The astronomer uses the light year as a measuring standard. This is the distance light travels in one year at a speed of 186,000 miles per second. We could not use the speed of light as a standard if light did not move at a constant speed.

Second, *light moves in a straight line*. When a beam of light strikes any solid object that is not transparent, it cannot move through it. The object casts a clear black shadow. Light cannot bend around corners. That is why we cannot see around corners. We can hear around corners because sound travels in air. And sound waves do move around corners. But light travels only in a straight line. We cannot see unless there is a straight clear path to the thing we are trying to look at.

Third, *light can be reflected*. We can see the moon because it reflects light from the sun. We can see ourselves in a mirror for the same reason. In fact, if light were not reflected, we could see nothing at all. For everything we see, except light itself - the sun and stars and light bulbs and fire - we see by reflected light. This ability to reflect light is made use of in a special kind of telescope, called a reflecting telescope.

Fourth, *light can be bent*. Light cannot move around a corner, but it can be bent. If you place a stick in a pool of water, the stick seems to bend where it touches the water. The light reflected from the stick is bent by the water. This is called refraction. Every telescope and microscope uses this principle. So do eyeglasses. They bend the rays of light and focus them in the right place. You can see how this works by looking at the figure. The ground glass bends the light rays. If it is ground properly, all of the rays are bent the same amount. This makes a clear picture which is larger and easier to see.

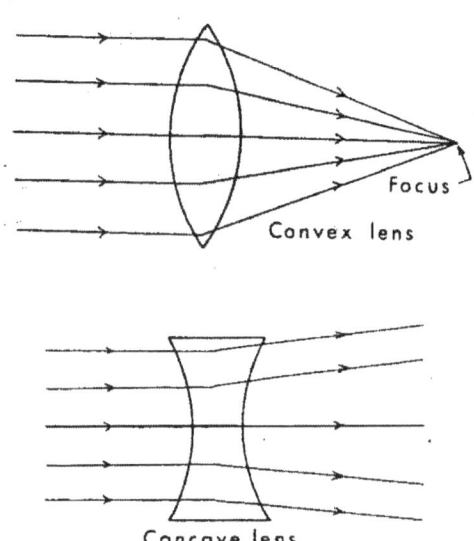

FIGURE   Refraction of Light Through a Lens.

Refraction of Light Through a Lens.

Fifth, *light is a series of frequencies*. Light radiates as a mixture of several frequencies, not as just one wave. Each frequency appears to our eyes as a separate color. Light is like a dozen radio stations all broadcasting on different frequencies. When we see, we tune in all of these frequencies at the same time. When we see one color, we see one of these frequencies. The others have been lost somewhere. We will learn more about this when we study color.
These five characteristics of light are used by scientists to study the universe.

The Optical Telescope

One way that astronomers have learned about the universe is by studying the radiations coming from the stars. The frequency they study most is light. Light can be studied through optical telescopes.

A telescope is designed to capture light from distant stars and concentrate it into a small area that can be seen and understood. Our eyes are very small, and only a little light reaches them at one time. The telescope gathers light from a large area and bends the light rays until they fit the small area the eye can see. This gives a brighter and stronger picture.

An optical telescope can use a mirror to gather light, or it may use a curved piece of glass called a lens. The amount of light that the telescope gathers depends upon the size of the mirror or lens. A telescope that uses a mirror to gather light is called a reflecting telescope. The mirror reflects the light that it gathers. A telescope that uses a lens to gather light is called a refracting telescope. The lens refracts, or bends, the light it gathers. A large mirror or lens gathers more light than a small one. Because a big mirror can be made more easily than a big lens, our largest telescopes are reflecting telescopes. The largest reflecting telescope in the world has a mirror two hundred inches in diameter. It is located on Mount Palomar in California. The lens of the largest refracting telescope is forty inches in diameter. It is located at Yerkes Observatory on Lake Geneva.

The Refracting Telescope

The small hand telescope is usually a refracting telescope. It uses a lens to gather light. The figure below shows a typical refracting telescope. Light enters the telescope through the lens in

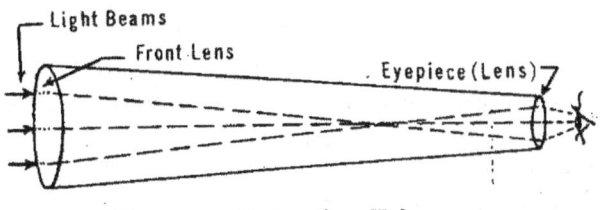

FIGURE   Refracting Telescope.

front. It is bent, or refracted, by the lens. This pulls the light together into a smaller pattern. The light rays cross over in the middle of the telescope. Then they strike the eyepiece and produce a smaller picture of the light entering the lens. This small picture can be seen by the eye. Because the light rays will have crossed, the picture as seen by the eye will be inverted, or upside down.

By placing a camera at the end of a telescope, instead of one's eye, astronomers are able to photograph the heavens.

Reflecting Telescopes

The lens in a refracting telescope must be ground perfectly smooth to prevent distortion. This cannot be done with very large lenses. The largest telescopes, therefore, must use the curved mirror to gather light. The light is reflected off the curved surface of the mirror and focused into an eyepiece.

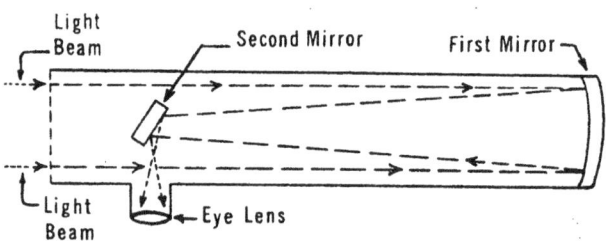

Using Telescopes

The amount of light gathered by a telescope depends upon the size of the lens or mirror it uses. A telescope with a thirty-six inch lens gathers about thirty thousand times as much light as the human eye. This shows the astronomer many more stars than his eye can see unaided. On a clear night you can look up and see a few thousand stars in the sky. But with a four-inch telescope you can see more than two million stars. The giant reflecting telescope on Mount Palomar shows billions of stars that are too far away to be seen by the naked eye.

The larger telescopes are able to separate the light coming from the different stars and give a clear picture of each one. This is called *resolving power*. It is very important to astronomers. One of the meanings of *resolve* is to *separate or break up into elements*. A cluster of stars may look like a blur of light in a small telescope. In a larger scope the blur of light is seen as many separate stars. The elements of the blur of light - the stars, that is - are resolved by the stronger telescope.

Thermocouple

Astronomers use the telescope more than any other tool available. But they also make use of other instruments. We have seen that the camera has helped astronomers make a record of the heavens. An instrument called the *thermocouple* is used with a telescope to measure the temperature of distant stars.

The Spectroscope

Another instrument, called the spectroscope, is used to show the type of material in different stars. Light from a star can be beamed into the spectroscope through any telescope. The light passes through a triangle of glass, called a *prism*. This prism bends the light rays. It bends every frequency a different amount. Thus it has the effect of separating the different frequencies of light coming from the star. Each frequency appears as a band of color in the spectroscope.
By learning the patterns of frequencies produced by different materials, the scientist has learned how to interpret these lines. From spectroscopic studies, we know that the sun is composed of many of the same elements we have on earth. In this way we have also learned the composition of many stars far away in the universe. We have found out that most stars are made of some of the same types of material we find here on earth.

The Radio Telescope

Radiation from the stars includes many frequencies that our eyes cannot see. In recent years scientists have begun to study these invisible radiations to learn more about the universe. The instrument they use is called a *radio telescope*. It is really a very powerful radio receiver with a special antenna. The signals received from space sound much like static on a regular radio. In fact, radio astronomy was discovered because of static caused by radiation from space. The astronomers have learned how to *tune in* broadcasts from outer space. Because the signals are very weak, a large antenna is used to strengthen them.

Inside the radio telescope, the faint electrical signals coming from space are *amplified*, or strengthened, thousands of times. The signals received by the telescope are recorded to give a permanent record. This record can be studied. When the *radio telescopes* pick up a source of large electrical radiations, scientists try to find the area with a large optical telescope. Sometimes the cause of the radiation can be seen. If so, the astronomers can interpret the signals they receive by radio. One astronomer has already taken a picture that shows two huge galaxies colliding or passing through one another. The collision produced very strong radiation signals. These signals were detected by a radio telescope. The astronomer located the area with the two-hundred-inch optical telescope and took the picture.

The radio telescope provides many advantages, once we learn to use it. It can *see* further into the universe. It can be used in the daytime. It is not bothered by clouds. Used with the optical telescope, the radio telescope is rapidly expanding our knowledge of the vast universe around us.

CHAPTER 2

STARS AND GALAXIES

Bodies in Space

Can you imagine a single star so large that it could hold a thousand million bodies the size of the earth? There are stars in the universe as large as that. We have nothing that we can compare them to. This is one of the problems we meet when we study the whole universe. Everything is so large and things move so fast that it is hard to comprehend them. Here on our planet a quart jar of earth contains billions, of billions of billions of atoms. In some parts of the universe, a quart jar would contain only one tiny atom. How can we imagine space that holds absolutely nothing? Space around the earth contains atmosphere. We cannot see it or feel it, but it is there all the same. Large areas in outer space contain almost nothing.

Even in the part of the universe we can see, the earth is only a tiny speck. Our sun is only one very ordinary little star among the millions of stars in the Milky Way. Most of the other stars in this galaxy are about the same size as the earth. Some are larger than the sun. Others are smaller than the earth.

Far out in space there are millions of other galaxies, some larger and some smaller than the Milky Way. We do not even know how many galaxies there are. Most astronomers believe that there are many millions of planets throughout the universe. But no one has seen any outside our own solar system.

Galaxies

Most of the matter in the universe is gathered together in great clusters called galaxies. Besides its millions of stars, the Milky Way galaxy also contains probably millions of planets. In addition, there are immense clouds of dust and gas spread around the galaxy. In fact, about half of all the matter in the universe exists in the form of dust and gas. Many astronomers believe that new stars, like the sun, are formed from these great clouds.

The galaxies are very large. It takes light hundreds of thousands of years to pass from one end of a galaxy to the other. Since the distance between galaxies is measured in millions of light years, there is very little danger of a crash. This is a good thing, because the galaxies move through space at terrific speeds.

Radiation

Every visible star in the universe produces radiation. Great amounts of energy are thrown into space by the atomic furnace inside each star. This radiation travels through space at the speed of light. Every part of the universe is filled with this radiant energy from stars. Planets like the earth catch and hold some of the energy from this radiation. We are able to live because the earth can capture from the sun this radiant energy which provides heat and plants for food.

Maybe other planets contain living things that use radiant energy to live, too. Since there are millions of stars, it is probable that many of them have planets similar to the earth. Far away in space, perhaps millions of light years from earth, another planet may hold people who look at our sun through their telescopes. We may never know whether they do for certain, unless they are fairly close to earth. No man could live long enough to make the journey.

Stars

The stars are the queens of the universe. The great heat and pressure inside the star raises the temperature to several million degrees centigrade. Atomic fusion takes place at this high temperature. Stars consume hydrogen nuclei, or use hydrogen nuclei to produce atomic energy. When four hydrogen nuclei are combined to form a helium nucleus, energy is released. This energy is radiated into space by the star. When the supply of hydrogen in a star is gone, we say the star dies. Our own sun will stop consuming all of its hydrogen someday. But no one needs to worry about that for a long time. There is enough hydrogen in the sun to last for millions of years.

The sun is a typical star. There are billions of other stars of roughly the same size and temperature. These stars are called *main sequence* stars. The sun is about 860,000 miles in diameter - just about average for main sequence stars. Inside, the temperature of the sun is about 20 million degrees C. Its surface temperature is much lower - about 6,000°C. About 99 percent of all the stars we can see are main sequence stars.

There are two other types of stars in the universe. One type is much larger than the sun, the other is smaller. The larger stars are called *red giants*. They are the real giants of the universe. These stars are cooler than the sun and radiate at a different frequency. Their radiation appears red in the spectroscope. That is why they are called red giants. Their size is really amazing. One red giant, called *Betelgeuse* (B-ē'tel jooz), is 25 million times as large as our sun.

The smaller stars are called *white dwarf* stars. They are much smaller than the sun and hotter. They are about the size of the earth. But the matter in white dwarfs is packed so tight that a cubic inch of the stuff has as much mass as a freight car full of coal. And they are exceedingly hot.

Inside A Galaxy

The large galaxy called the Milky Way, where we live, looks something like the one shown in the figure below. The galaxy in the picture looks like a giant pinwheel in a firework display. Not all

galaxies are shaped this way. Some are a round cluster of stars. Some are shaped something like an H. The large galaxies, like the Milky Way and *Andromeda*, are spiral galaxies. In a spiral galaxy the stars are grouped together in the long curved arms of the spiral. There are several million stars in just this one galaxy. Our galaxy covers the distance of a hundred thousand light years from one edge to the other.

Scientists do not know exactly how many stars there are altogether in the universe. One astronomer estimated that there were 10,000,000,000,000,000,000,000. There is no way that we can compare this number on earth. The galaxies are usually spinning as they speed through space.

All galaxies that we can see are filled with great clouds of dust and gas. Many astronomers believe that new stars are born inside these clouds of dust. We know that some stars are young and others are old; so we are certain that the stars were not all produced at the same time. A star lives by *burning* hydrogen and producing helium. By... measuring the amount of helium, we can tell how long a star has been burning. Some stars are much older than others. In fact, some stars have probably burned out long ago. Others have gathered themselves together for one last effort and exploded.

How can a cloud of gas form a new star? The answer lies in the movement of the cloud of dust and gas and in Newton's law of gravitation. The movement of the gas and dust creates powerful currents inside the cloud. This tends to bring particles together. The area where the particles are crowded together then has a larger mass than other parts of the dust cloud. According to Newton's law, the attractive force of a body depends upon its mass. Slowly, the mass of gas and dust grows larger and heavier. The larger and heavier it grows, the more its mass increases. This attracts still more gas and dust.

These clouds are extremely large. Some are millions of millions of miles across. The rotation of the cloud mass tends to pull it into the shape of a ball. The dust and gas at the outer edge of the ball are drawn toward the center by the pull of gravity, thus increasing the pressure on the particles inside the rotating ball. The increase in pressure increases the mass and creates an even greater pull from the outside toward the center. This causes the temperature to increase. When the temperature gets high enough, an atomic reaction occurs. The cloud, now a solid mass of tightly packed dust and gas, begins to burn. A new star has been born.

This explanation is only a theory of how stars are made. No one has ever seen a star made this way. The process probably takes thousands or millions of years. It does seem to explain the facts that we know at this time. This theory is accepted by many scientists as the best explanation we have for star making.

shows an explosion that took place more than nine hundred years ago. The gases and matter are traveling from the explosion at a rate of six hundred miles per second. You can imagine how far they have traveled in nine hundred years. Yet the explosion still looks small in our telescopes. This will give you an idea of how far away the explosion took place.

When a star explodes, the explosion is called a *nova*. It is not unusual in the universe, where there are billions of stars. Some of them stop burning and explode every few years. Once in a while, however, there is a real super explosion called a *super nova*. The figure shows one of these extra-large explosions. Scientists know about a half dozen of them in the last thousand years. The energy that is released in one of those explosions is so great that to compare it with a hydrogen bomb would be like comparing the sun with a tiny spark.

Explosions

When a star uses up its supply of energy, it stops burning. Some stars go out in a blaze of glory. They pull themselves together and explode with a tremendous bang. The figure below

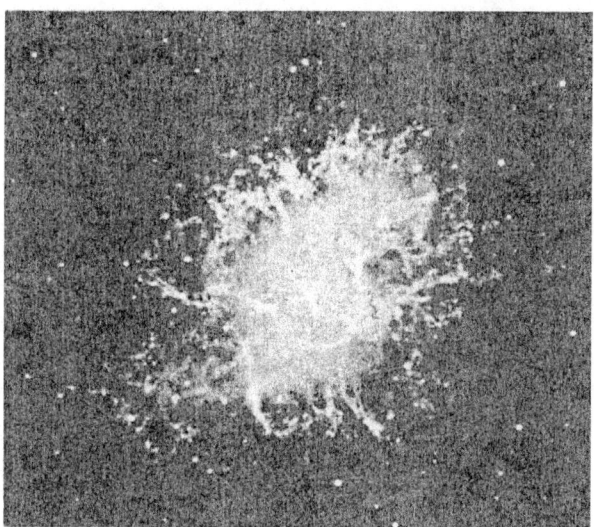

Most scientists do not believe that our sun will explode. They think it will just fade out and stop burning. It may flare up strongly before it stops burning. If it does, the earth will be burned to a crisp before it turns into a cold solid ball.

Questions About The Universe

There are many questions about the universe that we would like to answer. How old is it? Where did it come from? Is the universe slowly thinning out, or is it growing more dense? As yet, scientists cannot answer such questions. Perhaps they may never be able to.

We try to estimate the age of stars by measuring the helium they contain. But each year our estimates grow larger. Long ago it was thought that the world was only a few thousand years old. Today we believe that the earth is about five billion years old and that many parts of the universe are much older than that.

Scientists have made many observations about the universe that they cannot explain very well. For example, galaxies far from the earth seem to be moving away at very high speeds. If these observations are correct, all of the matter in the universe must have been lumped together some billions of years ago. Some scientists believe that a great explosion tore the universe apart about five billion years ago and started the galaxies moving away from each other. This is called the *big bang* theory of the universe.

Other scientists do not accept the *big bang* theory. They believe that the universe has been manufacturing new matter at a *steady pace*. This is called the steady state theory of the universe. Both theories explain some of the facts we have. Neither theory explains all the facts. So the chances are that both theories are somewhat wrong. This will give you an idea of the kinds of problems astronomers must try to solve.

Some of our difficulties in solving them come from the limited scope of our instruments. The whole universe is so large that there is probably much that we cannot see in the limited range of our telescopes. The earth's atmosphere also makes observation difficult. Many scientists hope that the new radio telescope will help solve some of our problems by *looking* deeper into outer space. Even if it does, there are more than enough problems to keep astronomers and physicists busy for many, many more years.

CHAPTER 3

THE SUN

If you look into the sky during daylight hours, you cannot see any stars except the sun. The glare of the sun's rays, dispersed through the atmosphere, makes it impossible for us to see the feebler light of the stars that are farther away. At night, when the sun is not shining on our part of the earth, we say the stars are *out*, forgetting that they have been there all the time. We sometimes forget that the sun is also a star. It is the closest star to earth, only 93 million miles away. We can see the sun very clearly; its light reaches us in about eight minutes. The star nearest us after the sun - named *Alpha Centauri* - is more than four light years from earth. That is about 25 trillion miles. So you can see that the sun is easier for us to study than any other star. Much of our knowledge of stars comes from studying the sun.

Facts About The Sun

The sun is a main sequence star about 860,000 miles in diameter. That is, its diameter is just over one hundred times the diameter of the earth. But this makes a much greater difference in volume. Both the earth and the sun are practically spherical. To find the volume of a sphere, we use the formula $V = 4\pi r^3/3$. Since $\pi = 3.1416$, to get just an approximate idea we can cancel out the π of the numerator with the 3 of the denominator. This gives us $V = 4r^3$. (That is not accurate, of course, but it gives a pretty close relationship.) So, Sun $V = 4 \times 430,000 \times 430,000 \times 430,000$; Earth $V = 4 \times 4,000 \times 4,000 \times 4,000$.

This shows that the sun has, roughly speaking, a million times as much volume as the earth. That is why we do not have to worry about the sun's running out of hydrogen fuel. It is so large that it can change vast amounts of matter into energy every second without a noticeable loss of mass.

The sun is all in a gaseous state. Temperatures on the sun are so high that we know it could not be in a solid state. We know that it has no solid crust, for parts of it turn at different rates of speed. If the continent of Africa, let us say, turned faster than the continent of North America, the earth's crust would break. On the sun, some parts do turn faster than others. The inside of the sun is probably made of hydrogen gas under great pressure. This hydrogen is consumed in the sun's nuclear furnace to produce energy and helium.

The Surface of the Sun

So the sun actually does not have a real surface at all. The face of the sun is a mass of gases hot enough to melt any metal we know. Iron and copper and the other elements found on the sun are all in a gaseous state because of the high temperatures.

The disk of the sun is called the photosphere. Above the *photosphere* is a layer of flaming gas from five thousand to ten thousand miles deep. This layer is bright red in color. It is called the *chromosphere*. It could be compared to the atmosphere of the earth because it surrounds the sun's disk. Outside it, there is yet another layer of gases called the *Corona*, which extends perhaps a million or more miles into space around the sun.

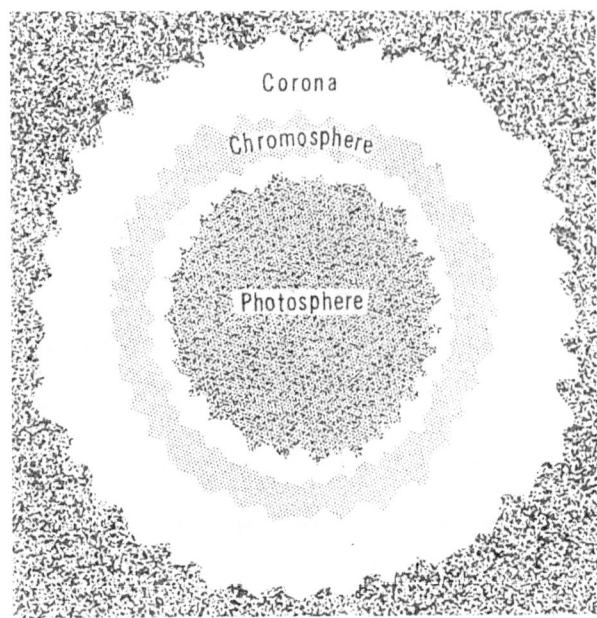

The temperature around the sun changes. Close to the surface, in the photosphere, it is about 6,000°C. Higher, in the Corona, the temperature rises, reaching as high as 1,000,000°C at times. Even this is much lower, however, than the temperature at the center of the sun, which is estimated at 20,000,000°C.

Solar Flares

The sun as we see it seems to be a smooth, flat disk. But pictures reveal it as a swirling mass of flaming gases. The surface is like the inside of a furnace. Flames leap out, and great columns of fire, called *solar flares*, jump thousands of miles into space. The figure below shows a large solar flare in action. The white dot shows the size of the earth. This explosion threw a sheet of flame 250,000 miles into space. When the sun *kicks up its heels* this way, even the earth feels the shock 93 million miles away. Great clouds of electrical particles rain down toward the earth. They rush into our atmosphere and cause electrical static and other interference with radio messages.

Inside the Sun

We can see only the surface of the sun. But by studying the surface we can learn something about the inside of the sun too. We now know that nuclear reactions are always taking place inside the sun, just as they occur inside a hydrogen bomb. This was not known until World War II. While looking for new military weapons, scientists found that the energy inside the atom could be released from certain elements. They learned how to split the nucleus of the atom. This, as you know, is called nuclear fission. Later, after World War II had ended, scientists also learned how to put together atoms to release even more nuclear energy by nuclear fusion. Nuclear fusion is the principle used in the hydrogen bomb. The sun, also, carries on nuclear fusion inside its surface. The temperature is very high, and nuclear fusion goes on continuously. The energy thus released is thrown off as radiation.

Every second the sun converts over *four million tons* of matter into energy. It has been using up this much of its matter every second for millions of years. Yet the sun is so large that only one millionth of one millionth of its mass is consumed in an entire year. The sun has an ample supply of fuel for a long time.

The Sun and the Earth

The sun is the most important star in the whole universe for us living creatures on earth. We would all die if the sun stopped radiating. Except for the small bit of atomic energy we produce and that from deep inside the earth, every bit of energy on earth comes from the sun. Green plants are able to use the energy from the sun to make chemical changes inside their own bodies. They trap the sun's energy and change it into plant material. Animals eat the plants and change plant material into animal material. Even the energy in coal and petroleum was once part of the sun. Plants that had stored solar energy in their bodies were changed - under great pressure through the ages - into coal. When we burn coal, we simply release energy that some plant took from the sunlight long ago. Only in an atomic reactor or through chemical reactions can energy be produced that does not originate in the sun.

A very small fraction of the sun's total radiation reaches us on earth. If much of it did, we would all be burned to a crisp. Only a few billionths of the sun's output falls on the earth's surface. This tiny fraction supplies the energy that warms our planet, moves the winds and the oceans, and grows our whole food supply. Without the energy from sunlight, no plant would grow, no rain would fall, and all of our water would quickly turn to ice.

Every minute millions of tons of water are lifted into the air by solar energy. This water is carried over the earth by winds, which are generated by solar energy. Thus, the sun's heat is distributed evenly over the earth. The sun is like the central unit in a giant air-conditioning system. It provides the heat that keeps us warm. It also runs the carrying system that circulates the heat. From no other source could we begin to replace the energy which the sun provides for us. All of the energy produced by a million atomic bombs would not equal the energy we get from the sun in just a few days.

Sunspots

Although we know a great deal about our own private star, the sun, there are still some things about it which remain mysteries to us. One of the most interesting of these mysteries is the occurrence of great whirls that appear on the surface of the sun from time to time. These whirls look like dark spots on the face of the sun. We call them *sunspots*. Close-up pictures show them as great whirling masses of gas that move across the sun's disk. There are usually two or three of them on the surface at the same time. They may last only a few minutes, or they may stay several weeks. Some are small - only a few miles in diameter. Others are larger than the earth. We know they are not hotspots, for the temperature is actually cooler inside the sunspot than on the rest of the sun's surface. We do not know why they appear. They seem to come in regular cycles. Every eleven years the number of sunspots increases rapidly. For a short time there are a great many large ones. Then the activity slows down again.

That is about all that we know about sunspots at this time. They have been watched and charted. Photographs of them have been taken. But why they appear or what they are remains a mystery. We do know that their effect is felt even here on earth. They seem to cause tremendous electrical storms in the atmosphere far above the earth. Radio signals often *fade out* at this time. Sometimes intercontinental radio is interrupted for several days. The *great northern lights, aurora borealis*, become active. These glowing streaks of electrical energy appear around the poles of the earth like giant streamers. Even on the surface of the earth, snowstorms and electric storms are more violent during a sunspot period than during normal times. Here is one of nature's mysteries, right on our own doorstep, that we have not been able to solve. There are also other questions about the sun that we have not yet been able to answer.

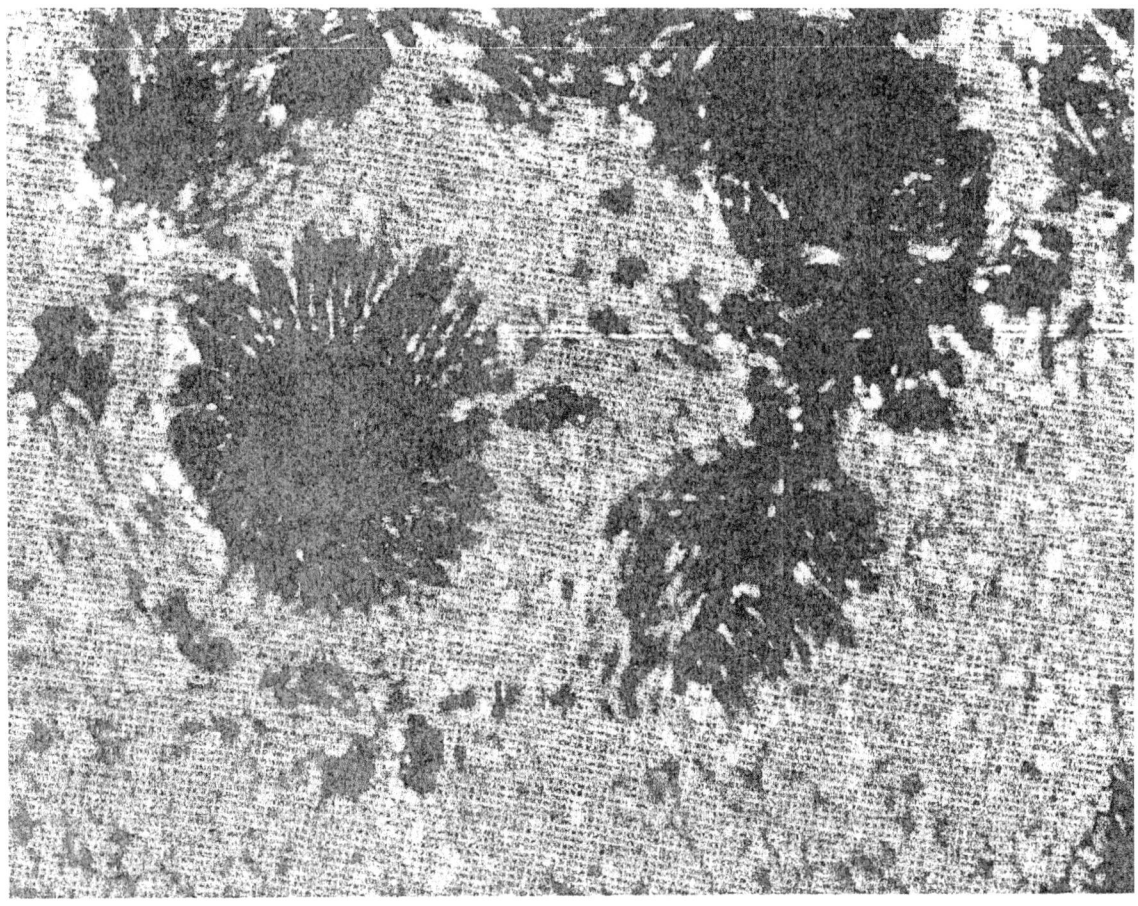

Using the Sun's Energy

When we buy gasoline, or coal, or food, we are actually buying energy to run our automobile, or heat our house, or keep our bodies alive. Such commodities are expensive, yet we must have energy to live. Every day the sun pours great amounts of energy onto the earth. Sunlight is free for everyone. Why cannot solar energy be used directly to do some of the jobs we use coal and oil for now? The answer is that solar energy can be so used, but it is often cheaper to produce energy by burning coal than to harness the energy of the sun. Nevertheless it is possible to use solar energy to cook, to heat houses, and even to make electricity.

If, on a hot summer day, you leave your car for a while with the windows closed, it becomes very hot inside. The car acts as a *heat trap*. Sunlight passes freely through the windows; it strikes the car seats and other parts of the interior; and some of the energy is absorbed, or taken up, by the material and changed into heat. The rest is reflected back out the windows. But a good deal of the heat inside the car cannot escape through the windows. Glass, which lets light in freely, is not a good conductor of heat. It is an insulator. Thus, much of the heat -is held inside the car, and the temperature rises steadily as the sunlight pours in.

If there is enough sunlight, this same principle can be used to heat a house. The top of the house can be covered with glass panes. Beneath the glass, the roof can be painted a dark color so it will absorb sunlight well. The sunlight passes through the glass and is absorbed by the black paint. The heat cannot escape through the glass. So the heat trap becomes very hot. Water can be circulated through this *heat trap*. The heat warms the water, which can then be circulated through the house to warm it. Actually water has been known to boil in a *heat trap* of this sort. But if the skies are cloudy and there is not enough sunlight, this system will not work well. It is used now in some homes in the southern United States, where there are many sunny days.

Another method of producing heat from sunlight is based upon the same principle as the reflecting telescope. A large reflector is used to concentrate the rays of the sun in a small area. When the sun's rays strike a pan placed in the center of the reflector, they are changed from radiant energy to heat energy. A reflector a few feet wide can boil water very quickly. By using reflectors more than a hundred feet in diameter, scientists can produce very high temperatures with the rays of the sun. Temperatures of several thousand degrees C can be produced if the rays are captured from a large area and concentrated into a small area.

Notice that sunlight is not heat. Sunlight is radiant energy. It can be changed into heat, which is another form of energy, if it is absorbed by the surface it strikes against. When we wear dark-colored clothing in the summertime, the cloth absorbs energy from the sun and changes it to heat. This is why people who live in warm climates wear light-colored clothing. Light-colored clothing reflects the sun's rays instead of absorbing them.

CHAPTER 4

THE SOLAR SYSTEM

The sun is the center of a system that contains many different bodies which orbit around it. The sun together with all its satellites is called the *solar system*. The largest of these satellites are the nine planets. The earth is one of these *nine planets*. As the earth circles the sun, it takes with it a satellite of its own, the moon. Several of the other planets have moons like ours also. These moons are all parts of the solar system too. So are the thousands of smaller bodies, called *meteors* and *comets* that orbit around the sun.

Most of the matter in the solar system - about 98 percent, in fact - is concentrated in the sun itself. Only 2 percent is found in all the rest of the bodies together. That is, the sun is fifty times as massive as all the rest of the solar system.

The Origin of the Solar System

Where did the solar system come from? How did these celestial bodies originate? These are questions that scientists have not been able to answer as yet. Scientists, called cosmologists, have been studying the question of the origin of the solar system for a long time. They have come up with several theories to explain it, but as yet they have not found one that all the experts in the field can accept. As new facts come to light, any theory has to be adjusted to contain them. If they will not fit, the theory has to be discarded. This has happened to several theories about the origin of the solar system. Cosmology offers a very good example of the way theoretical scientists work. They must constantly revise their ideas to fit new knowledge as it is revealed.

Three theories of the origin of the solar system seem to be supported by more scientists than others. They are worth a brief explanation. It will give you an opportunity to see how scientists form their hypotheses. One is that long ago a giant star passed near the sun. The force of gravity drew a great mass of gaseous matter out of the sun. As the star passed by, this mass of matter escaped from union with the sun and formed, instead, a series of rings around it. Then the escaped gases condensed into liquid and finally into the solid planets and other bodies that we know in the solar system.

The second theory proposes that there were once two suns. Since most stars seem to live in pairs, this is a reasonable guess. The theory then assumes that the second star exploded. After the explosion, the earth and other planets were formed from the matter that remained. A variation on this theory is that the second star never became formed actually. Instead, the gas from the second star was distributed through space and was formed into the planets and moons.

Another theory, once very popularly believed, is that the solar system was once a mass of dust and gas. The gases condensed, and the star that we call the sun formed in the center. The material that remained outside the central body formed the planets and other members of the solar system.

The Present Solar System

Although we do not know how the solar system began, we do know what it looks like at the present time. There is the sun in the center of the whole system. The sun is one star, held in place in a very large galaxy called the Milky Way. Around the sun, there are the nine planets and thirty-one moons, as well as thousands of small planets called *asteroids*. There are, also, millions of chunks of matter called *meteors*. And there are millions of clusters of frozen particles called comets.

You can see the pattern of the solar system in the figure below. We are looking down at the top of the system in the drawing. Each planet has an orbit, or path around the sun, that it follows regularly. The sun alone radiates heat in the solar system. All other members of the family are dead bodies that obtain their heat from the sun.

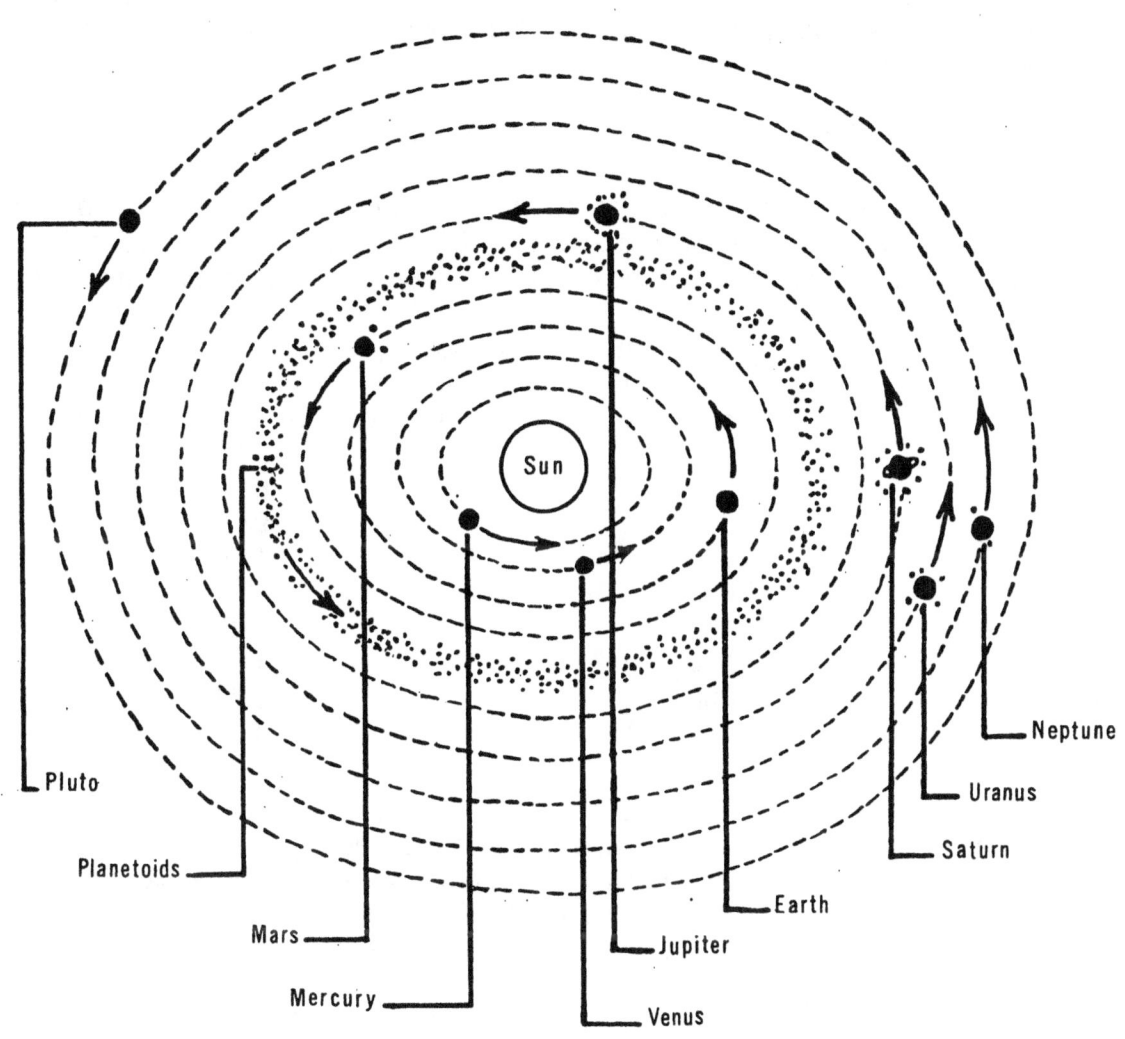

The Planets in the Solar System

We can see the planets because they reflect light from the sun. Five of the planets (Mercury, Venus, Mars, Jupiter, and Saturn) can be seen with the naked eye. The others must be viewed through a telescope and even then they are not easily spotted. The one that is farthest from the sun, Pluto, has been photographed through a large telescope. But little is known about it.
The sun is not in the exact center of the orbits of the planets. For example, the earth in one part of its orbit comes within 91 million miles of the sun; but in another part the two are nearly 94 million miles apart. The orbits of the other planets, too, are not quite circular. They are elliptical. That means they are like circles stretched out.

The Size of the Planets

The chart that follows shows the diameter of each planet and the distance from the planet to the sun. Notice that there are two groups of planets. Mercury, Venus, Earth, Mars, and Pluto are much smaller than the four large planets Jupiter, Saturn, Uranus, and Neptune. The four large planets are called *Jovian* planets. They are four to eight times as large as the earth in diameter. The smaller planets are called *terrestrial* planets. *Terrestrial* means *like the earth*. These smaller planets are all about the same size as the earth.

A Closer Look at the Planets

Since we live on a planet, it is interesting to see what the other planets in our solar system are like. Actually, none of them are much like our own. Mars is probably the most like Earth of all other planets. Each one is different from the others in climate, appearance, size, and many other features.

Chart of Planets

Name	Diameter (miles)	Distance from the Sun (million miles)
Mercury	3,100	36
Venus	7,900	67
Earth	8,000	93
Mars	4,200	142
Jupiter	88,600	483
Saturn	74,100	886
Uranus	32,000	1,782
Neptune	31,000	2,793
Pluto	(not known)	4,000 approx.

Mercury, which is closest to the sun, is the smallest, coldest, hottest, and fastest planet, in the solar system. It moves around the sun at a speed of about twenty-three miles each second. Every eighty-eight days it completes one rotation and one revolution. Thus its day and year are of equal length. Its movements are such that the same side is pointed toward the sun at all times. Because Mercury is only 36 million miles from the sun, the side facing the sun is very hot. The side away from the sun is very cold. The temperature averages about 400°C on the hot side, and about -200°C (200° below zero) on the cold side. You can see that life as we know it cannot possibly be found on Mercury.

The largest planet in the solar system is Jupiter. This large body spins very rapidly on its axis. Every ten hours Jupiter makes one complete revolution. It has a day ten hours long instead of twenty-four as that of Earth. The distance around the equator of Jupiter is almost eleven times that of Earth.

Venus and Saturn are very beautiful planets. Saturn has broad white rings around its equator. These rings, two bright ones and a fainter inner one, are tiny particles caught in the gravity around this planet. The particles orbit around Saturn like a well-disciplined parade. This produces the band effect you can see in the figure below. Venus is one of the brightest objects in the night sky. This planet is covered with a solid mass of white clouds, which reflect light very well. Venus is warmer than Earth, but its temperature is not so high as that of Mercury.

Pluto, the loneliest planet, was not discovered until 1930. We know that Pluto is about the same size as Mercury and that it is very cold because it is so far from the sun.

Mars

Since we live at the beginning of the space age, the planet Mars is most interesting to us. Mars is the first planet that man has visited. Mars is more like the earth than any other planet in the solar system. It has clouds, and it has some atmosphere. There is probably some water on Mars too, since the poles appear to be white during the cold season, suggesting that snow and ice form there just as at the North and South Poles of the Earth. Most of Mars seems to be a dry desert area. Parts of Mars change color during the year. This may mean that there is plant life of some sort on the planet. Some people believe that animal life may exist on Mars too, but this seems less likely.

In 1877 a number of long straight lines were discovered on Mars. These are the famous *Schiaparelli's Canals*, named for the Italian astronomer who discovered them. The lines are so long and straight that people believed that they had been built by some animal. But astronomers think that the *canals* are not manmade at all. Clouds obscure our view of Mars, and no one is certain what the dark lines really are. The problem could be solved easily by landing on Mars or even by taking a photograph from a close distance. This was a3complished in the late 90's with our unmanned landing on Mars.

Moons

We are all familiar with our own natural satellite, the moon. We will study it in detail in the next chapter. You may not know that there are thirty other moons in the solar system, some larger than ours. Mars and Neptune have two moons each. Jupiter has twelve. Saturn has nine, and Uranus five. Six of the moons are larger than ours. In fact, four of Jupiter's moons are nearly as large as the planet Mercury. These moons are not very important in the solar system. Our moon is chiefly responsible for the tides, and it does reflect some light to the earth at night. We do not know what effect the other moons in the solar system may have on their planets.

Since 1957 the earth has been presented with several new moons, or artificial satellites. Some of these satellites are in orbit for just a short time and then plunge back to earth. Others will remain in orbit almost indefinitely. These artificial satellites also help us learn more about the universe. Already they are used for weather prediction, navigation, communication, and many other uses. They have also provided us with information about radiation in the space beyond our atmosphere.

Comets and Meteors

A comet is a chunk of matter made up of frozen particles and gases. The main body of a comet is usually about one mile in diameter. We think of a comet as an object with a long *tail*. But this tail is present only part of the time. While the comet is far out in space, it has no tail. When it approaches the sun, the heat melts the frozen material and releases gases. These form the comet's long tail we see so often. This tail may be thousands of miles long. One very famous comet, called Halley's Comet, was first sighted long before Christ was born. Halley's Comet was last in our area in 1986. Its orbit brings it back to the sun once every seventy-six years. The comet is visible for several days as it orbits near the sun. Then it heads back into space, losing its long white tail and freezing solid again.

Any piece of solid matter flying through space is called a meteor. There are millions of meteors in the solar system alone. Most of them are about the size of a pea. A few are large and heavy and weigh many tons. Astronauts will have to worry about these meteors when they leave the earth's protective atmosphere. Every day thousands of meteors strike the earth. These fallen meteors are called *meteorites*. When they enter the atmosphere, friction between the meteors and the air molecules produces heat that burns all but a few of the meteors. Those that strike the earth are usually made of iron or rock. Some of these meteorites are quite large. The Barrington Crater in Arizona was made by a meteorite. This crater is one-half mile wide and about five hundred feet deep. Another large meteorite landed in northern Russia. The noise was heard for hundreds of miles. Trees were knocked flat for miles around the crater. The meteor dug a great hole in the earth and buried itself.

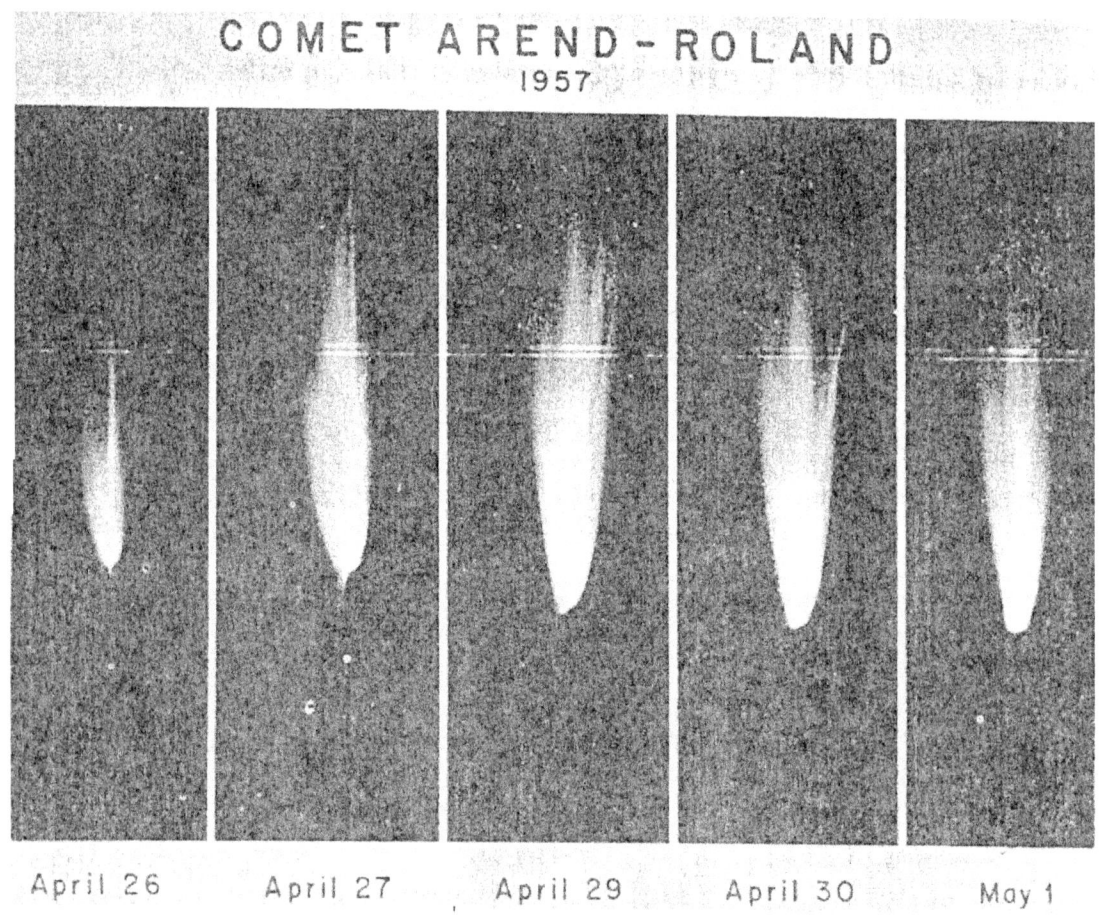

CHAPTER 5

THE MOON

The earth's one natural satellite we call the moon. This satellite orbits around the earth just as the earth orbits around the sun. Many scientists believe that the moon was once part of the earth. They believe that ages ago it was torn from the part of the earth where the Pacific Ocean basin now is.

But a good many scientists do not accept this theory. They believe that the moon was formed separately. Neither theory can be proved at this time.

Size and Location of the Moon

The moon is a sphere, or round ball, about two thousand miles in diameter. It is, roughly speaking, 1/60 as large as the earth. The moon's orbit is about 240,000 miles from earth. It makes one complete circuit in 27 1/3 days. Like the earth, the moon also rotates on its axis as it travels its orbit. It, too, makes one full rotation every twenty-four hours. Since both the moon and the earth rotate at the same rate, the same face is always directed toward the earth.

The moon seems to be made of the same elements we find on earth. That is why some people believe that the moon was once part of the earth. Since the moon is the smaller, it does not have as much attraction for other bodies as the earth does. The mass of the moon is less than that of the earth. For this reason your weight, if you were on the moon, would actually be only 1/6 of your weight on earth. Since your muscles would be the same, you could probably break the world high jump record just hopping up and down.

Man landed on the moon in 1969 and returned several times.

Phases of the Moon

In the night we can see the moon shining in the sky. But we know that the moon is a dead body like the earth. It does not radiate energy. It shines by the reflected light of the sun. Since the moon moves around the earth and the earth moves around the sun, we cannot always see the

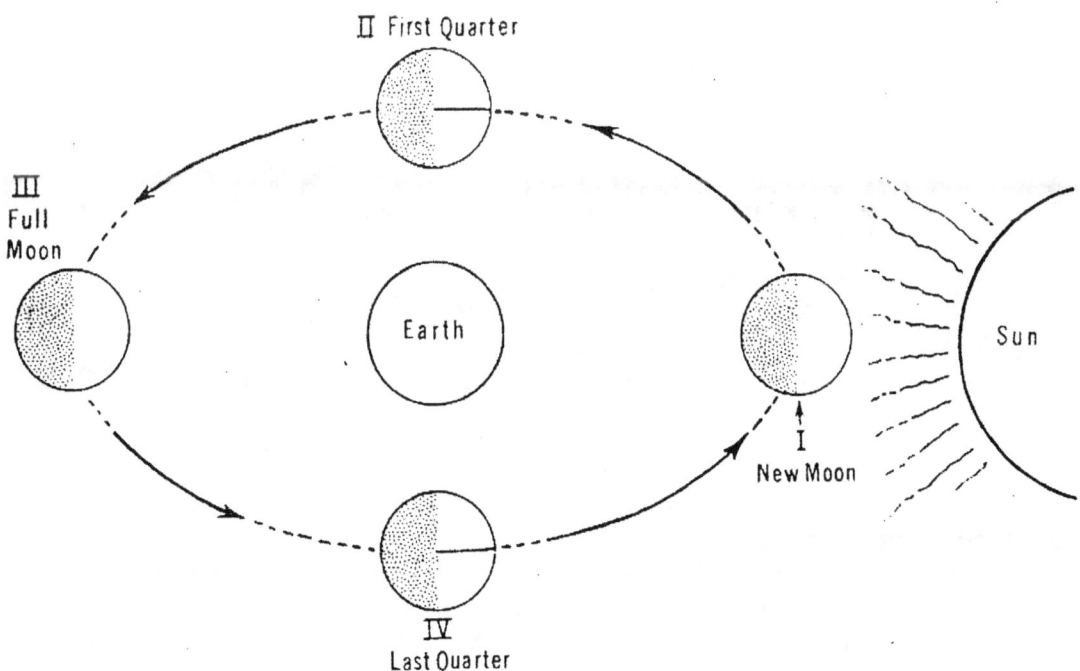

moon. In parts of the orbit, the moon comes between us and the sun. When it does, only a small part of the moon can be seen from the earth. These changes in the amount of light reflected from the moon are called the *phases of the moon*. The part of the moon we can see depends upon the relative position of the moon, the earth, and the sun.

In step I of the figure above, the moon is between the sun and the earth. The side of the moon facing the sun is lighted. But this side of the moon cannot be seen from the earth. Therefore, the moon appears to be dark because the side toward the earth is not lighted by the sun. This is called the *new moon.*

The moon continues to orbit around the earth, moving counterclockwise. That is, it moves in the opposite direction to the hands on a clock. When the moon reaches step II, 1/4 of its lighted surface can be seen from the earth. This is called the *first quarter* of the moon.

In step III, the earth is between the moon and the sun Now we can see the full face of the moon. This is called *full moon.* It the exact opposite of a new moon. After full moon, the moon gradually appears to grow smaller and smaller until it disappears once again in a new moon period. Of course, the moon does not stop at each step in the drawing. It passes through these four positions as it moves around the earth. As it looks to us, the moon seems to grow from a thin sliver to a full moon and then to fade away to a thin sliver again. You can see the face of the moon in the figure below as it appears during the full moon and two quarters.

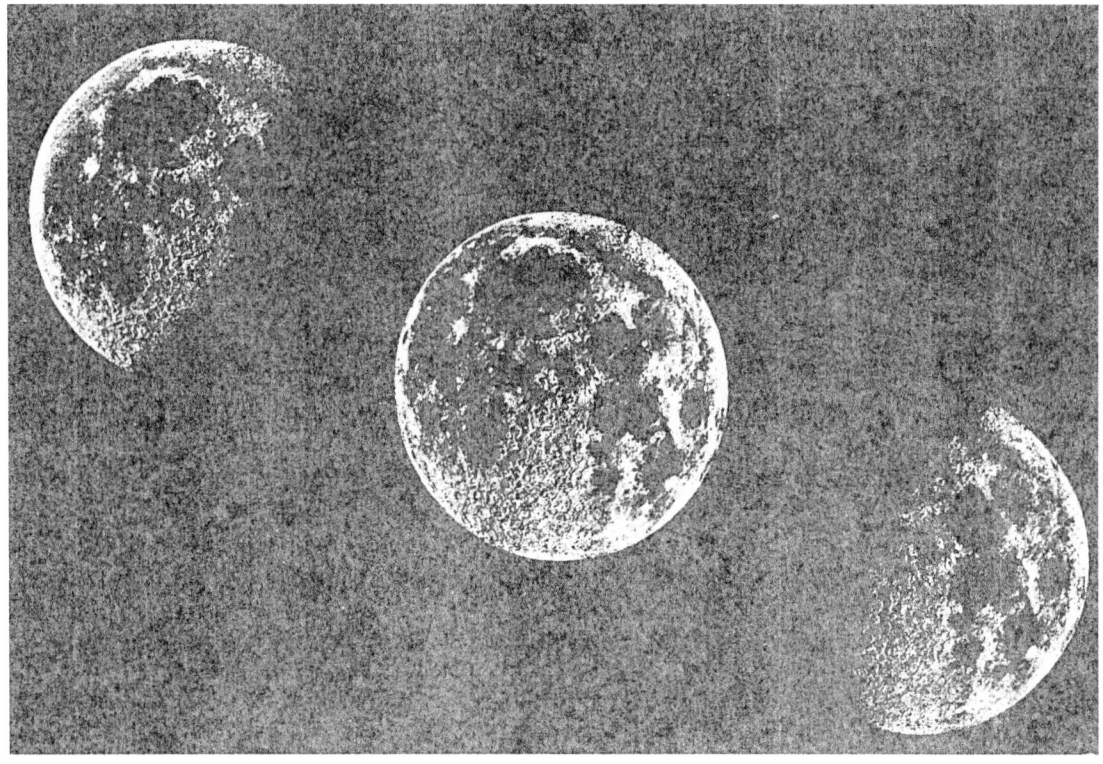

The Surface of the Moon

Look closely at the surface of the moon in the figure above. Notice the great pits and holes in the surface. These scars are probably due to meteors striking the moon. There is no blanket of atmosphere on the moon, and so the surface gets the full force of any meteor that hits it. Another possible cause of these pits could be volcanic activity. Some astronomers believe that at some time the moon may have had some great explosions that tore up its surface. One reason why the craters are hard to explain is that they are so large. We do not have pits and craters of this size on earth.

The mountains on the moon have peaks as high as those here on earth. Some of them are more than 25,000 feet high. Because there is no air or water on the moon, there is no wind and no rain. You could probably feel sound vibrations on the moon with your feet, but there would be no vibrations against your eardrums because there is no air to carry the sound. So there would be no sound except that carried through the solid parts of the moon. Since there is no weather on the moon, there is no erosion except for that caused by falling meteorites. The surface of the earth is worn away by the action of wind and water and glaciers. On the moon, the surface remains almost unchanged. The mountain peaks are high and sharp. They have not been worn down like our mountains on earth.

The surface of the moon was thought to be covered with a thick layer of dry powder or dust. The surface is solid rock with many craters caused by meteorite impact. Some were as little as three feet across.

Temperature on the Moon

A weatherman on the moon would have an easy job. Every day is clear, sunny, and hot. Every night is dark and very cold. The side of the moon facing the sun is hot. In fact, the temperature is 100°C, hot enough to boil water. The dark side of the moon is cold. Usually the temperature is -130°C, or 130° below zero. The temperature on the moon drops very quickly when the sun goes down. In a few hours the temperature might drop nearly 200° on the centigrade scale. This drop has been measured during an eclipse. As the earth moves between the sun and the moon and cuts off the sunlight, the temperature in the shaded area of the moon falls rapidly.

Eclipses

When the earth moves between the sun and the moon, it casts its shadow on the moon. Light travels in a straight line and it cannot bend around the earth to light the moon. When the moon moves between the earth and the sun, the moon's shadow falls on the earth. Within the shadow, the sun cannot be seen. Since the moon is smaller than the earth, its shadow covers only a small part of the earth's surface. Outside this shadowed area, the sun is bright and clear. Inside the shadow, the sun is blotted out by the moon. This shadow period is called an eclipse. When the earth blots out the moon, we have a *lunar eclipse*. When the moon blots out the sun, we have a *solar eclipse*. A lunar eclipse occurs about every six months. Several years pass between total solar eclipses.

A Lunar Eclipse

Every month the earth moves between the sun and the moon. But it does not always cause an eclipse. Sometimes the earth's shadow falls above or below the moon and there is no eclipse. When the earth's shadow does strike the moon, we have a lunar eclipse. A lunar eclipse is shown in the figure below. The earth, sun, and moon are all in a line. The shadow of the earth covers the moon. No light from the sun strikes the moon and, therefore, no light can be reflected. We cannot see the moon at all in lunar eclipses.

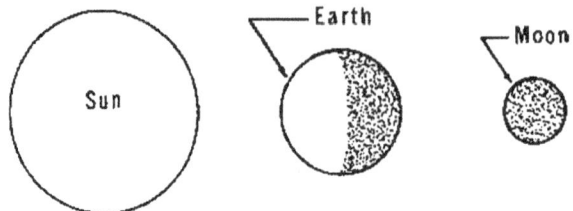

A Solar Eclipse

When the moon comes between the earth and sun, we have a solar eclipse. In a small area on earth, perhaps a hundred miles square, the sun is then completely blotted out. The position of the three bodies is shown in the figure below. A total eclipse lasts only a few minutes. The location from which the total eclipse may be seen changes. A total solar eclipse was visible from the state of Maine in 1963 and another was visible from Florida in 1970. After 1930, there will be no more solar eclipses visible from the United States until the twenty-first century. The location of an eclipse is known many years in advance. We also can know of those long past, because the motion of the solar system is regular so that we can calculate when they occurred.

Solar eclipses have been very useful to science. As the sun is blotted out by the moon, scientists can study the sun's surface more carefully. Einstein's theory of relativity was first tested during an eclipse. He predicted that the mass of the moon would bend the light rays from the sun. His theory was proved to be correct. The theory plays a vital part in the scientific study of the universe.

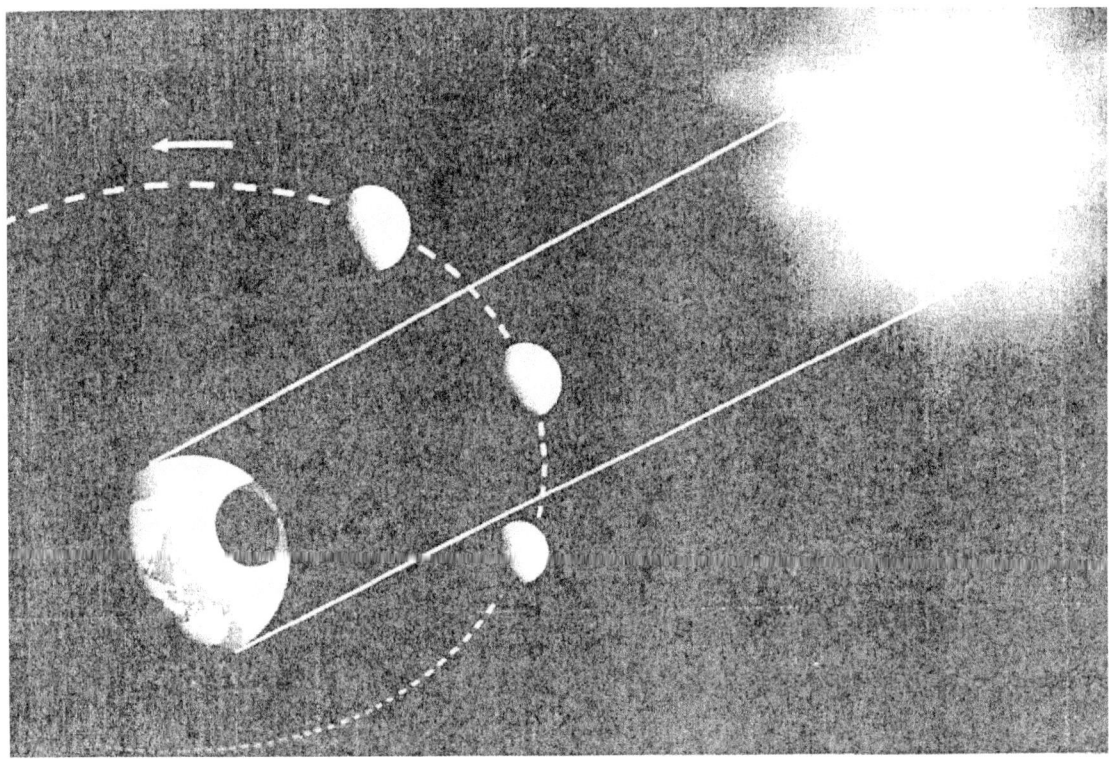

Tides

Anyone who lives in an ocean harbor knows what an important part the tides play in ocean shipping. The chief cause of tides is the moon. The attraction of the moon for the earth causes the water on earth to rise toward the moon. This creates a bulge in the oceans that follows the moon around the earth. When the bulge reaches shore, we have tides. During a tide the water level may rise several feet and then fall back once again as the moon passes. Some harbors in the world can be used only when the water level is at high tide. By their rise and fall the tides help clean out the bottom of the harbors.

Although the sun and moon are the main cause of tides, the shape of the shoreline and the depth of the ocean also affect tides. Some parts of the world have little or no tides. Other areas have tides that raise the water level twenty feet or more each day.

CHAPTER 6

THE EARTH

Suppose an astronomer outside the solar system could tell us how the earth looks to him. What would he say? First, he would tell us that the earth is a dead body and not a star. The earth is a planet of the sun, moving-around it in an orbit that is nearly a perfect circle. The sun is not exactly in the center of the circle, and the earth is closer to the sun in January than in July. Our astronomer would say that the earth is just over eight light-minutes, or 93 million miles, away from the sun. He would then go on to describe the clouds he sees and the water on the earth's surface. He would probably not mention people, since it would be hard to see anything this small. An elephant standing on the moon could not, be seen from the earth even with a powerful telescope.

The Planet Earth

The earth is like the other planets in the solar system in some ways. It is almost spherical in shape. It moves counterclockwise around the sun, as the other planets do. It also depends upon the sun for its energy supply. The earth spins on its axis, but not at the same rate of speed as the other planets. The earth is not quite spherical, as it is flattened slightly at the top and at the bottom. The length of a line drawn around the earth and through the poles is about sixty miles less than one drawn around the Equator. The difference is due to the polar flattening at the top and at the bottom of the earth. Three-fourths of the earth is covered with water. The. rest is dry land. But in many areas only a small part of the dry land is actually used.

The earth differs from the other planets in some important ways. It has an atmosphere that contains free oxygen. The atmosphere, as well as the surface of the earth, contains a great deal of water. Millions of plants and animals live on the earth and in the oceans. Unlike most of the other planets, the earth has climates and temperatures that support plant and animal life.
Movement of the Earth

Even when we stand perfectly still, we are moving through space in three directions at once. As part of the earth, we move with the surface as the earth spins. As part of the solar system, we also move in an orbit around the sun. And, finally, as part of the Milky Way galaxy, we follow the sun as it sweeps along in its place in the Galaxy. We take part in all of these movements whether we like them or not. We are so accustomed to our environment that we do not even notice the motion. The two movements of the earth that concern us most are the revolution of the earth around the sun and the rotation of the earth on its axis. These two movements give us day and night, the seasons, our calendar and time system, and a measure of distance.

Measuring Time

As you have learned, the earth makes one complete turn on its axis every twenty-four hours. This gives us our standard for time. The day is divided into twenty-four equal hours, which contain altogether 86,400 equal parts called seconds. The spinning of the earth thus supplies our standard clock.

For years, we were unable to check the accuracy of our natural clock. But today we know that it is actually slowing down. The earth does not turn quite as rapidly as it once turned. Every thousand years, it loses forty-five minutes of time. This slowdown is due to the force of the tides. When they work against the earth's rotation, they absorb some energy from the earth.

The earth makes one complete trip around the sun in one year. During the year, the earth turns on its axis 365¼ times. Our calendar is meant to keep track of days and years. But, since it contains only 365 full days in four years it loses the four quarter-turns of the earth, or one full day. So we add one day to the calendar every four years. The year with the extra day is called *leap year*. Actually, even leap year does not make the calendar completely accurate. The earth does not make exactly 365¼ turns in one year. So we really would need to make another even smaller correction to keep the calendar perfectly right.

Time Zones

If you roast a piece of meat over an open fire and use a spit to turn it, you know that each part of the roast passes over the fire as the spit is turned. The earth is like a roast on a spit. Each time it turns, it passes under the heat from the sun, and we are kept warm by the sun's heat. The earth makes one full turn every twenty-four hours. So each hour, it turns 1/24 of the total distance around the earth. Now the earth is a globe and the total distance around any globe is 360 degrees. So the earth turns 1/24 of 360 degrees in one hour. Thus, we can say that the surface moves fifteen degrees in one hour.

Look at the figure below. The globe has been divided into fifteen degree units. If the sun is exactly over the line marked A, it will be exactly over B in one hour and exactly over C in two hours. The earth spins from west to east. So we know that a city at point A on the globe would see the sun overhead exactly one hour before a city on line B. And the city on line B would see the sun exactly one hour later than the city on line A

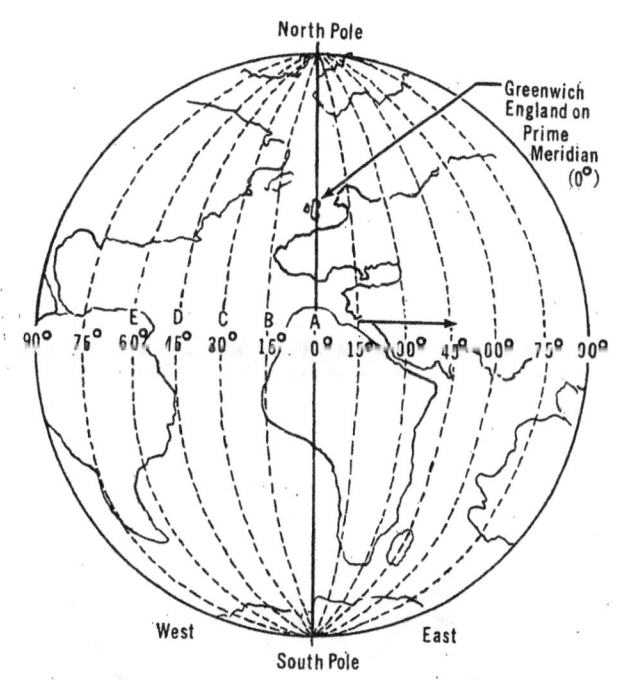

To keep all of the clocks on earth in time, we have divided the earth into twenty-four slices, each slice fifteen degrees wide. We have agreed that the time within each slice, or zone, will be considered exactly one hour different from the time in the next. Four of these time zones fall within the United States. The time zone on the east coast is exactly three hours ahead of the one on the west coast. The lines that divide the time zones do not fall exactly upon the meridians. They are drawn to avoid cutting through large cities and heavily populated areas.

The Prime Meridian

When the earth had been divided into the twenty-four time zones, we still had to decide at which zone the day was to begin. This was decided by international agreement. The day begins when the sun crosses the line drawn through the North and South Poles and the town of Greenwich, England. This line is called the *prime meridian*. The line is drawn completely around the globe. When the sun is exactly over the line on the opposite side of the earth from Greenwich, the day begins. When the sun is exactly over the line drawn through Greenwich, it is exactly noon at Greenwich. This is the standard for time throughout the world. Every time zone sets its watch by the Greenwich zone. The New York City time zone is always five hours behind the Greenwich zone. The Los Angeles time zone is eight hours behind Greenwich time.

The International Date Line

With twenty-four time zones and a prime meridian, we have solved most of our problems. But one time problem still remains. Suppose a pilot leaves Chicago in a jet plane. He flies westward toward the sun and chases it all around the earth. When he lands in Chicago, he has been flying in daylight throughout the trip. No night has fallen, and he may think he is coming back to Chicago on the same day he left. This would not be true, since night would have fallen in Chicago before he returned. The question is: when did he pass into the next day?

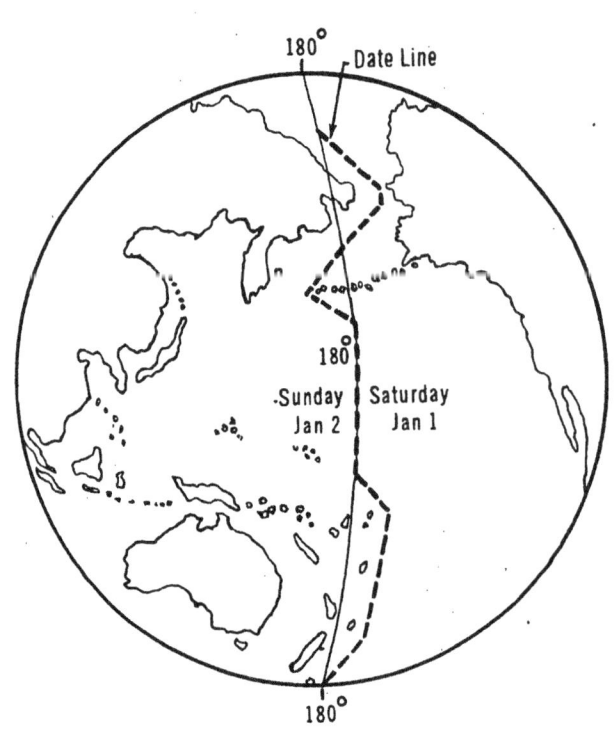

This problem is solved by drawing a line through the Pacific Ocean on the globe. We call this the international date line. Any traveler crossing this line from east to west must add one day to his calendar. Any traveler crossing the line from west to east must subtract one day from his calendar. This solves the problem for our jet pilot. When he crosses the line, he adds one day to his calendar. When he returns to Chicago, his calendar tells him that one full day has passed since his departure.

You will notice that the date line does not follow the meridian exactly. It is drawn, as all other zone lines, to avoid cutting through thickly populated areas.

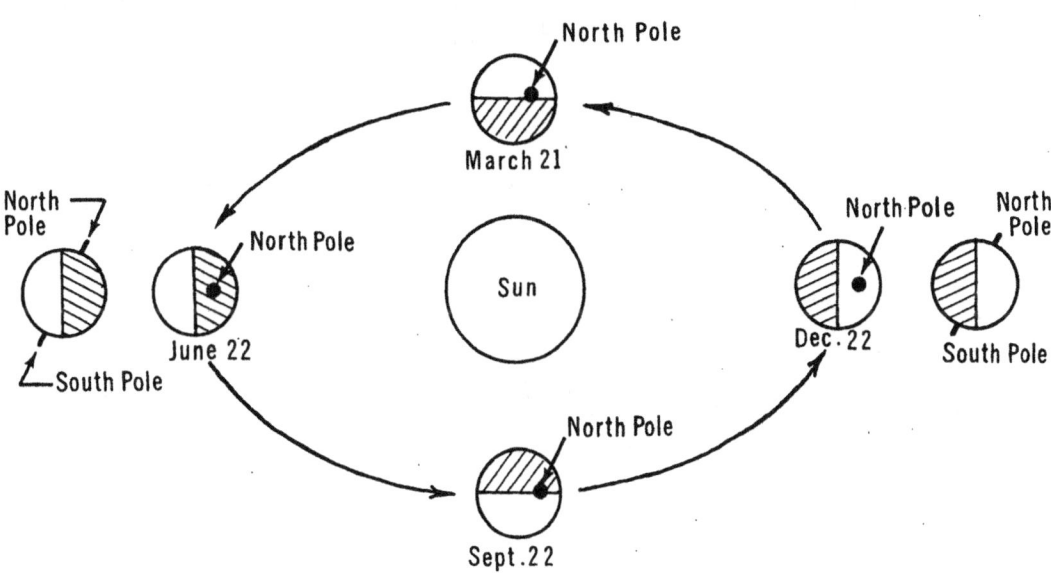

The Seasons

In the Temperate Zone where the United States is located, each year brings four seasons. In the northern United States, the difference between these seasons is striking. Winter is followed by spring, then summer, and then fall. The climate changes from cold to warmer, to hot and then to cooler as the change in season takes place. Why do these changes take place? There are two connected reasons. First, the earth moves around the sun in its orbit once each year. But this alone will not make the difference. Nor does the distance between the earth and the sun matter. The reason the seasons change is that the earth is not in an upright position. It is tilted to one side. The earth remains tilted in the same direction as it moves around the sun. It is this tilting, together with the movement around the sun that gives us a change of season.

Look at the figure below. Notice how the earth is tipped to the right. It is 23½ degrees from a vertical, or up and down, position. On June 22, the earth is tilted toward the sun. The North Pole is exposed to the sunlight and the South Pole is hidden. The northern half of the earth receives more sun during this period than the southern half. So it is summer in the Northern Hemisphere.

North Pole

From June until September, the earth continues its counterclockwise journey around the sun. On September 22 it is 90° from its original position in June. It is still tilted in exactly the same direction. The sun can now reach both the North and South Poles. From the earth, the sun appears exactly over the Equator.

By December 22 the earth's position is exactly opposite to what it was on June 22. The North Pole is now tilted away from the sun. The South Pole is exposed to the sun. And the Southern Hemisphere obtains more sunlight than the Northern Hemisphere. It is now summertime in Australia. Notice that the sun cannot reach the North Pole during this period. That is why there is total darkness during the winters and sunlight throughout the summers at the poles. During the winter, the sun cannot rise because its rays are cut off from the North Pole by the curve of the earth.

On March 21 the sun is back opposite its position of September 22. Both poles are lighted by the sun, which appears directly over the Equator.

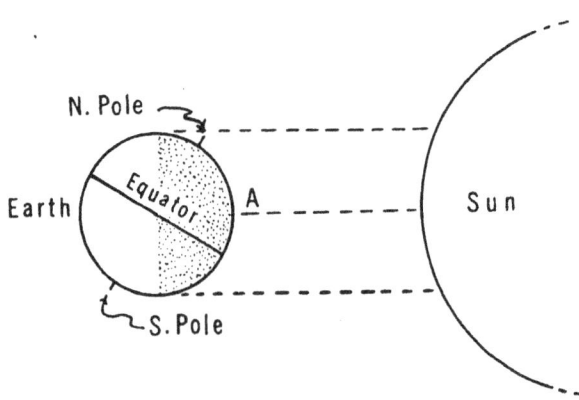

You can see this better in the figure above, which shows the relation between the sun and the earth on June 22. Notice that the sun's rays cannot reach the South Pole because of the curve of the earth. Notice also that point A, where the sun's rays strike directly on the earth, is far north of the Equator. At point A the sun would appear to be directly overhead. If you try to picture the tilted earth revolving around the sun, it will help you to see why there is no sunlight at the poles during the wintertime.

You can prove that the tilt of the earth causes the seasons by using an orange to represent the earth and a piece of wire for its axis. Stick the wire through the two poles and move the orange around an electric light bulb as though it were making an orbit around the sun. Watch the shadow caused by the electric light. You will find that you can see exactly how the seasons work by this simple experiment.

One View of the Earth

In this chapter, we have taken a look at the earth as a planet. In the solar system the earth is just one body orbiting around the sun. Because of the distance from the sun and the rotation, the climate on the earth changes from season to season. Because of the rotation of the earth, we have periods of day and night. The movement of the earth serves man as a clock and a calendar.

This is only one way of looking at the earth. We can call it an overview or look at the whole solar system. In the next few chapters, we will look at the earth from another standpoint. We will try to learn what the earth is made of and how it changes. We will study the effect of wind and water on the earth's surface. This is a view of the earth that is more familiar to us. But we must remember that the earth is part of the universe. It is also part of the solar system. It must behave according to the rules of the universe. We cannot change the way the earth takes part in the movement of the solar system. The next best thing to do is learn how the earth acts in the solar system and use this knowledge to plan our own work on earth.

Astronomy Notes and Resources

Origin of Life on Earth:

Panspermia:
Proposed by Savante Arrhenius
Main Idea: Life comes from elsewhere (other planets / other solar systems)

Possibilities:
- Spores of life can travel trough space (on meteorites)
- Life was "planted" on earth

This does not explain how life formed in the first place!

Organic Molecules formed in Meteorites:

Complex Organic Molecules found in Meteorites

Produced **abiologically** by **Fischer – Tropsch reaction:**
$$CO + H + catalyst \Rightarrow Organic\ Polymer$$
Produces **left-** and **right handed** amino acids!

Life on Earth uses only **left handed** amino acids.

Pre-Biotic Synthesis on Earth

Conditions on Primitive Earth:
- Reducing Atmosphere
- Warm Oceans
- Energy Sources

Urey Miller Experiment
Goal: Simulate Conditions on Primitive earth
Result: Organic Compounds can be produced

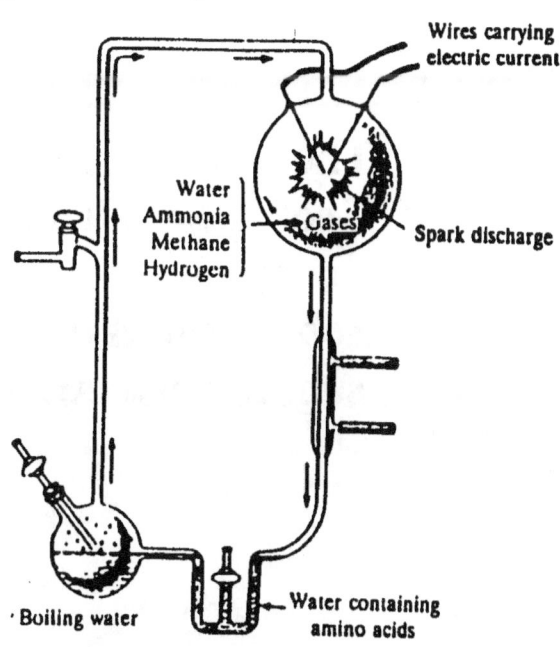

EVIDENCE THAT THE DINOSAURS BECAME EXTINCT BECAUSE OF A METEORITE IMPACT

C-T Boundary – a change in fossil records corresponding to some sort of mass extinction.

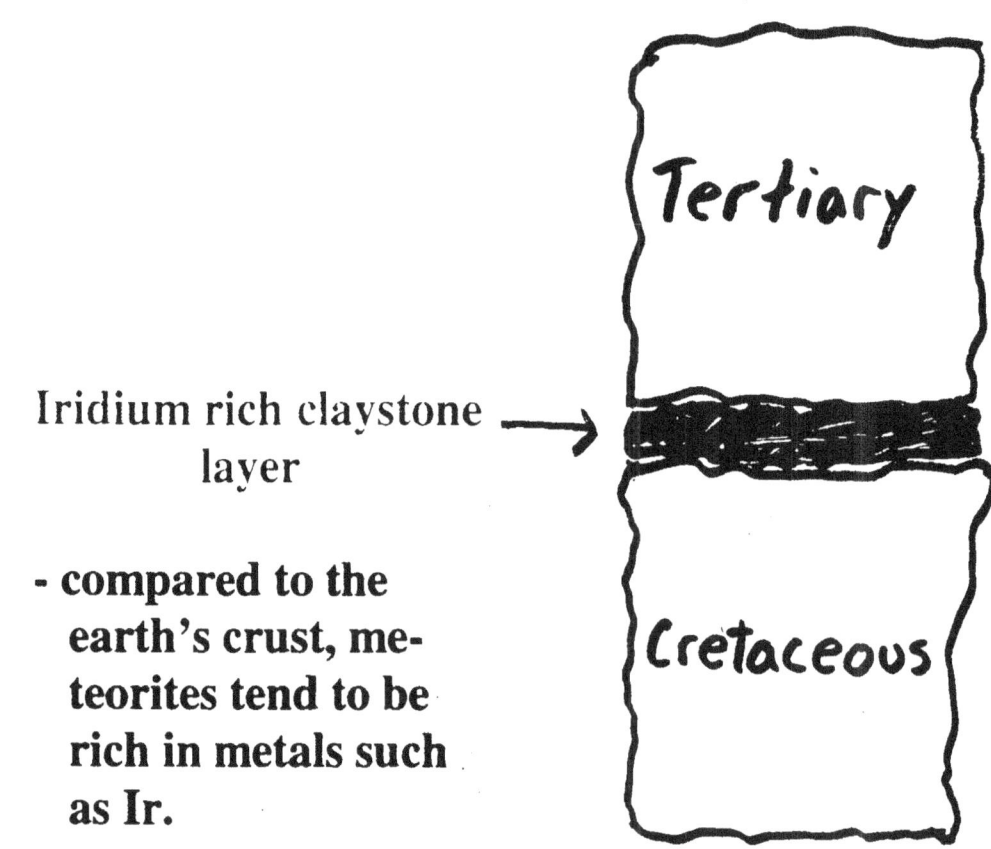

Iridium rich claystone layer

- compared to the earth's crust, meteorites tend to be rich in metals such as Ir.

Other Evidence:

- The Yucatan Impact Crater
- Geologic evidence of tidal waves
- Soot in the claystone layer suggests widespread fires

LIFE ON MARS

Arguments For:

- CO_2 and N_2 atmosphere

- Existence of H_2O

- Earth and Mars had similar *early* histories

- A meteorite of Martian origin showed that Mars once had liquid water and organics.

Stronger Arguments Against:

Today, organic molecules on the surface are destroyed by:

- UV Radiation

- Reactive, oxidizing molecules

Too cold to maintain liquid water

VIKING LANDER EXPERIMENTS

<u>PR Experiment</u> – looks for assimilation of atmospheric Carbon.

    Procedure – Martian soil samples were mixed with labeled gases and UV light

    Result -- Soil absorbed gases

<u>LR Experiment</u> - looks for metabolism by life-forms

    Procedure – Martian soil samples moistened with a labeled nutrient mix.

    Result - Organic compounds were re-released as gases.

<u>GEX Experiment</u> – looks for organisms' waste gases.

    Procedure – Martian soil samples mixed with organic-rich solution and a simulated Martian atmosphere.

    Result - "Waste gases" were emitted from the soil.

ALL THESE RESULTS CAN BE EXPLAINED BY AN OXIDIZING ATMOSPHERE.

Especially since the gas analyzer, or GCMS, found no organics.

REQUIREMENTS FOR A HABITABLE PLANET

A <u>moderate mass</u> that

    - is large enough to retain an atmosphere

    - is small enough to avoid being a gas giant

A <u>short rotation period</u> to avoid temperature extremes.

A <u>small eccentricity</u> to keep temperature variations small.

A <u>moderate distance</u> that places it in the star's ecosphere.

Ecosphere – the space around a star where liquid water can exist.

REQUIREMENTS FOR THE STAR OF A HABITABLE PLANET

O B A [F G K] M

Sun

Big stars have lifetimes that are too short.

A planet around a small star would be tidally locked.

WAYS OF DETECTING OTHER PLANETS

Direct Observation – actually seeing it

Eclipse Photometry – observing brightness variations

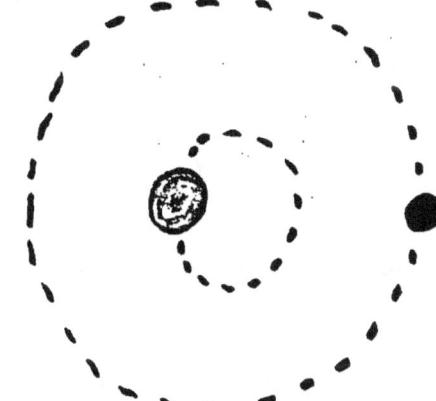

Astrometry – seeing a star wobble

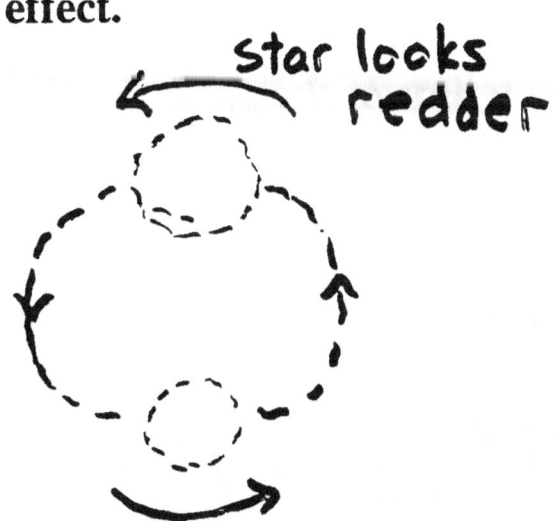

Radial Velocity – detecting a star wobble through the Doppler effect.

DRAKE EQUATION

Drake said that you can estimate the total number of communicating civilizations, N, in the galaxy today by multiplying:

- Total number of stars in the galaxy

- Fraction of stars with long enough lifetimes

- Average number of planets per star

- Fraction of planets that can support life

- Fraction of planets where life actually develops

- Fraction of life-inhabited planet that evolve into intelligent civilizations

- Lifespan of a communicating civilization, L.

and then divide by the lifetime of the galaxy.

If you do this you find that:

PLANETS

```
         INNER        (Asteroid Belt           OUTER
    TERRESTRIAL,       in between )         GIANT, JOVIAN
     EARTH LIKE                              /    |    \
    /     |     \                      very big  not so big
MERCURY VENUS EARTH MARS            JUPITER SATURN URANUS NEPTUNE PLUTO
   ☿     ♀    ⊕    ♂                   ♃      ♄      ⛢       ♆       ♇
```

Mercury (☿):
- old surface (craters)
- no atmosphere
- magn. field

Venus (♀):
- young surface
- spins backwards
- thick atmosphere (CO₂)
- no magn. field

Earth (⊕):
- young surface
- N₂ atmosphere
- magn. field
- one big moon

Mars (♂):
- old surface
- CO₂ atmosphere
- no magn. field
- two small moons

Jupiter (♃):
- largest planet
- cloud belt/zones
- one narrow ring

Saturn (♄):
- clouds not prominent
- wide complex rings

Uranus (⛢):
- no heat source
- no clouds
- high obliquity
- thin dark rings

Neptune (♆):
- clouds
- internal heat source
- big moon

Pluto (♇):
- rock + ice
- probably KBO
- thin atmosphere (N₂, CH₄)
- big moon

{ ☿ } no moons, slow spin
{ ♀ } dense, iron core, rocky mantle
{ ⊕ } ~24 h spin
{ ♂ } mostly rock

{ ♃ ♄ } solar composition — fast spin, internal heat source, strong magn. field — Fluid planets, no solid surface

{ ⛢ ♆ } solar composition + CH₄, NH₃, H₂O — slower spin, offset magn. field

{ ♇ } rock, H₂O ice — double sync. spin

CHEMICAL CONDENSATION MODEL (LEWIS)

Assume Cameron model

Condensation depends on pressure and temperature

⇓

condensation sequence depending on the distance from the Sun

refractory oxides:
CaO, Al_2O_3 ...
Fe, Ni (metals)
Mg, silicates (rock)
  } refractories (condense at high T)

H_2O (water)
NH_3 (ammonia)
CH_4 (methane)
  } volatiles (condense at low T)

↑ closer to the Sun

- Inner planets mostly made of rocks and metals
- Volatiles condensate only in outer Solar System
  → Giant planets: rock/ice cores + accreted gas
  → their moons: some rock + ice
                some ice only

KEPLER'S LAWS

① The orbit of a planet forms an <u>ellipse</u> with the Sun at one focus.

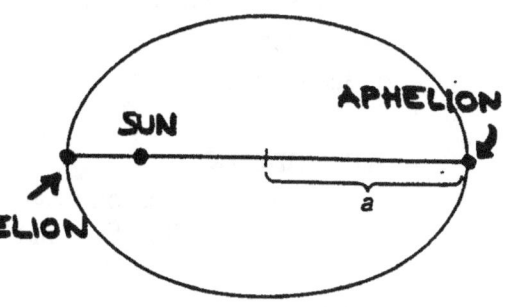

② The line joining the Sun and a planet sweeps out <u>equal areas in equal times.</u>

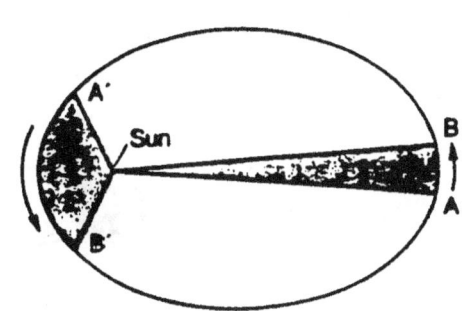

③ The square of the period of revolution of a planet is proportional to the cube of the semimajor axis of its elliptical orbit.

$$\frac{P^2}{a^3} = \text{constant} = \frac{4\pi^2}{GM_\odot}$$

P = period of revolution
a = semimajor axis
$G = 6.67 \times 10^{-11}$ m³ kg⁻¹ s⁻² gravitational constant
$M_\odot = 1.99 \times 10^{30}$ kg

If P is measured <u>in years</u> and a <u>in AU</u>, we can use the following expression:

$$\boxed{P^2 = a^3}$$ (only for the Solar System)

Aphelion distance = $a(1+e)$
Perihelion distance = $a(1-e)$

a = semimajor axis
e = eccentricity

Mars (Red Planet):

R=3400km
ρ=3.9 g/cm^3

Appearance:
- RED surface, Oxidized Material, Darker and Brighter Regions
- Clouds: White CO_2 and Water Clouds, Dust Clouds

Orbit and Seasons:

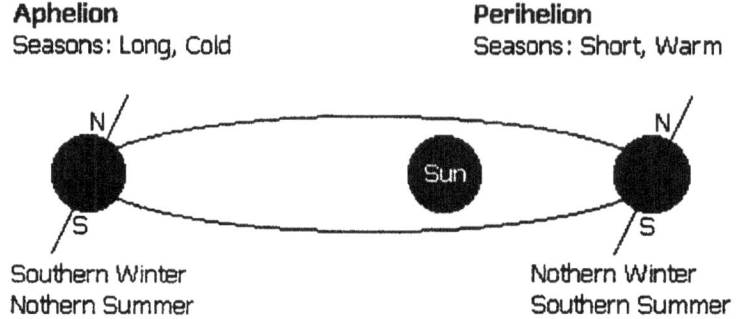

Aphelion
Seasons: Long, Cold

Southern Winter
Nothern Summer

Perihelion
Seasons: Short, Warm

Nothern Winter
Southern Summer

Eccentric Orbit: e = 0.09
- ⇨ Mars gets $1\frac{1}{2}$ more heat at perihelion
- ⇨ Seasonal asymmetry! (Strong Dust Storms during southern Summer)

Atmosphere & Seasonal Cycle:
Surface Conditions:
- Atmosphere **95% CO_2** other gasses: N_2, Ar
- Pressure: 6mb
- Temperature: 240K(day) 150K(winter polar cap)

CO_2 Cycle:
- Poles are Covered with Water Ice all Year
- Low Temperatures at Poles in Winter
- ⇨ CO_2 Freezes out
- ⇨ CO_2 Polar Cap / Pressure Variations
- ⇨ Spring / Summer Polar Cap resublimates
  (South Polar Cap retains some CO_2 frost)

Geology:
Hemispheric Dichotomy:
- Southern Half: Old Cratered Uplands
- Northern Half: Younger Volcanic Plains
- Large Impact Basins (Hellas)
- Volcanic regions
  Ex: Tharsis with Olympus Moons (largest volcano 25km high)
- Valles Marineris: Rift system

Water on Mars:

Today:
- Mars is Cold and Dry
- Small amount of Water as Vapor in Atmosphere
- Pressure too Low for Liquid Water (only Vapor or Ice possible)

Evidence for Water:
Petal-Shaped Ejecta Blankets
Outflow Channels:
- Large & Long
- Old: 1-2 b.y. of Martian History
- From Southern Highlands flowing to Northern Plains

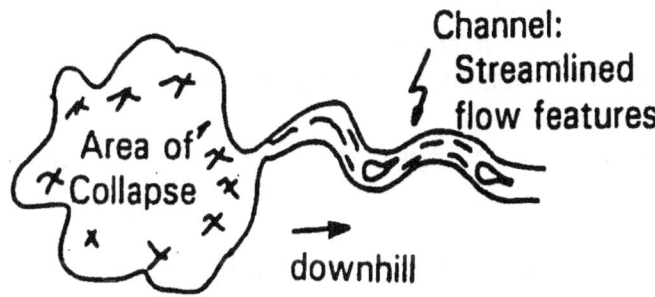

- Caused by: Underground Melting of ice
- ⇨ Water flows out (catastrophic flooding)
- ⇨ Terrain lost support from underground water
- ⇨ Collapses (Chaotic Terrain)

"Valleys":
- Small
- Very old
- Only in Southern Highlands
- Stubby Endings
- Caused by: Evaporation of Exposed ice
- ⇨ Headward Sapping

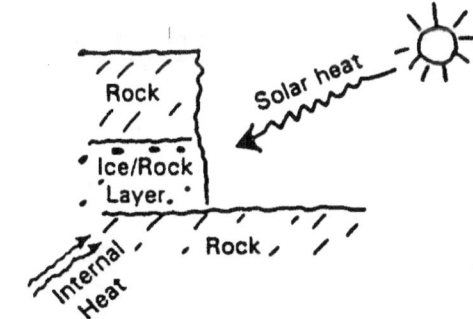

With time ice evaporates or melts.

Planetary Climate Changes:

Causes:
- Change in Solar Flux (Energy received from the Sun)
  Sun shines at very constant rate: variations < 1%
- Variations in e (eccentricity) of the planet's Orbit
- Variation in Obliquity (tilt of the pole)
- Precession (change in pole direction)
  Eccentricity & Obliquity changes, Precession caused by other planets (Jupiter for Mars)

Evidence for Climate Changes on Mars:
- Dry Channels (Outflow Channels)
⇨ There must have been liquid water at one time
- Layered Deposits near Poles
⇨ That means smaller changes happen (timescales 10^5-10^6 Yrs)

Conclusions:
- Mars had short period of better climate 3-4 billion years ago
- Then became like today / not much change

Test for Total of Gasses on Mars: Argon Test
- Argon is Inert (doesn't react) and Heavy (doesn't escape)
⇨ Outgassed Argon still in Atmosphere
- Assume ratio of outgassed Gasses same on Earth and Mars
- So we measure the Amount of Argon
⇨ That tells us the Total Amount of Outgassed Gasses
⇨ Findings: **Mars never had a Thick Atmosphere**

Differences Mars ⇔ Earth ⇔ Venus

Main Assumptions:
- Earth, Venus, Mars outgassed same gasses / and same relative proportions H_2O, CO_2, N_2
- Subsequent changes in the atmosphere depended on distance to the Sun (different initial temperature)

Evolution of Planets:

Venus:
- Too Hot for liquid Water
- ⇨ Water dissociates by UV light
- ⇨ Hydrogen escapes / O_2 Oxidizes Rocks
- ⇨ CO_2 main constituent in atmosphere (N_2 second)
- ⇨ Greenhouse effect (heat trapped under clouds) heats up the planet

Proof Venus lost lots of Water: Measurements of D/H ratio

Earth:
- Water can become liquid
- ⇨ Oceans
- ⇨ CO_2 dissolves in Water, forms Rocks
- ⇨ Leftover N_2 main gas in atmosphere (O_2 produced by photosynthesis (life))

Mars:
- Water freezes
- ⇨ Ice
- ⇨ CO_2 main constituent in atmosphere (N_2 second)

But much less outgassing than Earth (shown by Argon measurement)

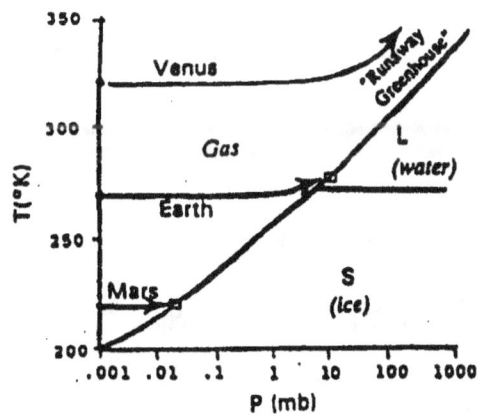

JUPITER AND SATURN

- Interior models based on
  - solar composition
  - ρ, M, R, oblateness
  - mass distribution

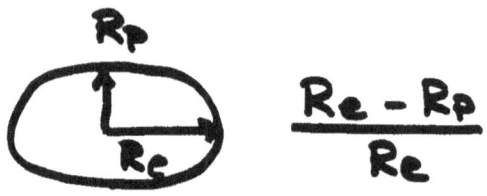

$$\frac{R_e - R_p}{R_e}$$

FLUID PLANETS, no solid surface, "solar-like" composition

At high pressure (3-4 Mbars): $H_2 \rightarrow$ metallic H + fluid state + rapid rotation $\Rightarrow$ magnetic field

- ♃ and ♄ both radiate MORE energy than they receive from ☉ $\Rightarrow$ internal heat sources:

  ♃ $\rightarrow$ heat stored from early contraction

  ♄ $\rightarrow$ He rainfall

CLOUD STRUCTURE

reddish BELTS
  (NH_4SH ammonium hydrosulfate)
whitish ZONES
  (frozen NH_3)

Belts/zones not conspicuous on ♄:
colder upper atmosphere ⇒ condense more NH_3 ⇒ thicker NH_3 haze

Below haze similar belt/zone structure to ♃'s

DIFFERENCES BETWEEN ♃ and ♄

- Saturn has less He in the atmosphere due to He rainfall (cause: lower interior T)

- Jupiter has stronger gravity ⇒ denser (more compression)

- Jupiter has a narrow ring (crumbling satellites). Saturn has wide, complex rings

URANUS and NEPTUNE

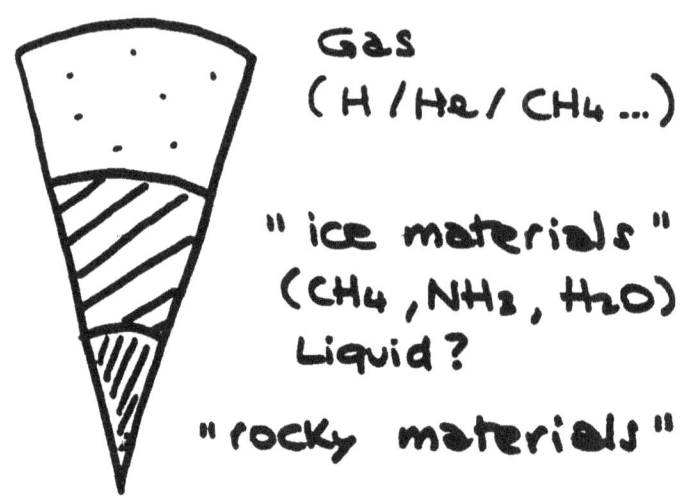

Gas (H/He/CH₄...)

"ice materials" (CH₄, NH₃, H₂O) Liquid?

"rocky materials"

Composition NOT solar (depleted in H, He relative to C, N, O), due to larger amount of CH_4, NH_3, and H_2O

- High pressure in "liquid mantle" → pressure ionized water
  ⇒ magnetic field

  OFFSET of magnetic fields → not centered on planet's center!

- Both ♅ and ♆ have narrow dark rings

DIFFERENCES BETWEEN ♅ AND ♆

- ♅ has no internal source of heat
- ♅ has virtually no clouds
- ♅ has very large obliquity (spins backwards

PLUTO & CHARON — PROBABLY LARGEST MEMBERS OF KUIPER BELT

HAVE ECCENTRIC, INCLINED ORBIT AROUND THE SUN
THEIR MUTUAL ORBITAL PERIOD EQUAL TO ROTATIONAL
→ DOUBLY SYNCHRONOUS SPIN   UNIQUE IN S.S.

COMPOSITION: PLUTO: 75% ROCK 25% ICE ; CHARON: ICE
SURFACE: PLUTO COVERED WITH CH_4 AND CO FROSTS
CHARON COVERED WITH WATER ICE
ATMOSPHERE: PLUTO HAS THIN CH_4 & N_2 ATMOSPHERE

KBO's — ASTEROID-SIZED OBJECTS BEYOND NEPTUNE
ORBITS WITH $a \sim 30-50$ AU, MOSTLY ECCENTRIC
SEVERAL DOZEN KNOWN, PROBABLY THERE ARE MORE
KUIPER BELT IS LIKELY SOURCE OF SHORT-PERIOD COMETS

CENTAURS — OBJECT ON ECCENTRIC ORBITS
BETWEEN JUPITER & NEPTUNE
HAVE CHARACTERISTICS OF BOTH COMETS & ASTEROIDS
BEST KNOWN IS CHIRON, WHOSE COMA HAS BEEN
OBSERVED CLOSE TO PERIHELION
CENTAURS HAVE UNSTABLE, SHORT-LIVED ORBITS
AND THEY PROBABLY COME FROM KUIPER BELT

SATELLITES OF JUPITER

- Small outer satellites
    - probably captured asteroids

- Small inner satellites
    - within Roche limit — source of ring particles

- GALILEAN satellites
    - planet-sized objects
    - NOT captured (formed together with Jupiter)
    - density ↓ with increasing distance from ♃ (→ Lewis)

Ganymede
- 1/2 ice, 1/2 rock
- strong magnetic field
- grooved terrain (evidence for expansion of crust)
- DIFFERENTIATED (source of heat: radioactive decay)

Callisto
- similar mass and composition
- uniform density
- no evidence of crust expansion
    - → UNDIFFERENTIATED
- heavily cratered surface

Europa
- water ice surface (very young) covered with cracks
- very low topography
- almost no craters
- indications of liquid water beneath ice (molten by tidal heating)?

Io

- Innermost Galilean satellite, similar in size to Moon
- Composition: Rock, just like our Moon
- Surface: High albedo, covered with SO_2 (orange)
- Active volcanoes detected on its surface
- Heat is supplied by TIDAL HEATING due to Io's eccentric orbits. Resonance with Europa & Ganymede keeps orbit eccentric.

ERUPTIONS
1. Explosive eruptions (plumes)
2. Effusive eruptions (flows)
3. High mountains → made of rock?
   → indicates basalt (rock) volcanism

Plumes can shoot materials hundreds of km high (due to low gravity and almost no atmo.)

Io is covered with sulfur because lighter volatiles have escaped (low G.) and sulfur is most abundant heavy volatile

Atmosphere: extremely thin, made of volcanic SO_2

Material from Io creates two toruses along orbit:
1. Torus of neutral atoms (exactly on Io's orbit)
2. Torus of ionized atoms (follows ♃ magnetic field)

Debris from Io can run into other moons: Amalthea, Europa

SATELLITES OF SATURN

- "Irregularly shaped" inner satellites
    made of ice, several associated with rings (shepherds or within gaps)

- "Round" inner satellites
    (Mimas, Enceladus, Tethys, Dione, Rhea)

- TITAN

- Outer satellites (Hyperion, Iapetus, Phoebe)

→ All (except Phoebe) have icy surfaces (H_2O ice)
→ No pattern of density with distance from ♄

Mimas	"death star": icy, only craters Causes Cassini Division
Enceladus	covered with cracks crustal expansion (tidal heating by ♄) probable source of E-ring particles
Tethys	in resonance with Mimas some cracks (very long Ithaca canyon)
Dione	the densest one, mostly rock some cracks and expansion (probably radioactive heating) in resonance with Enceladus
Rhea	largest icy satellite heavily cratered, no cracks
Hyperion	"tumbling", irregular, non-synchronous
Iapetus	albedo dichotomy: leading hemisphere dark (dust), trailing hem. bright (dirty ice)
Phoebe	retrograde, dark surface probably captured

TITAN

- ONLY MOON IN S.S. WITH REAL ATMOSPHERE
  COMPOSITION: SOME ROCK, SOME ICE
  SURFACE: UNKNOWN, COVERED WITH DENSE CLOUDS
  ATMOSPHERE: 90% N_2 AND 10% CH_4, PRESSURE 1.5 BAR
- HAS NO MAGNETIC FIELD.
- REDDISH COLOR OF THE ATMOSPHERE COMES FROM COMPLEX ORGANIC MOLECULES
- SUCH MOLECULES ARE CREATED BY UV LIGHT FROM SUN SOME OF THEM PROBABLY SINK TO SURFACE
- MAYBE THE SURFACE IS COVERED WITH LAYER OF LIQUID ETHANE, FORMING EITHER OCEAN OR LAKES BUT HUBBLE IMAGES SEEM TO INDICATE SOLID SURFACE
- TITAN IS INTERESTING FOR EXOBIOLOGY BECAUSE IT MAY BE MUCH LIKE EARLY EARTH (REDUCING ATMOSPHERE AND UV RADIATION)
- IMPORTANT DIFFERENCE: SURFACE TEMPERATURE IS ONLY 90 K SO THERE COULD BE NO LIQUID H_2O
- ORGANIC MOLECULES CERTAINLY PRESENT, BUT WE DON'T EXPECT LIFE ON TITAN
- TO BE EXPLORED BY HUYGENS PROBE IN 2004.

TRITON

- LARGE SATELLITE OF NEPTUNE ON RETROGRADE ORBIT
- PROBABLY OBJECT CAPTURED FROM KUIPER BELT

COMPOSITION: 75% ROCK, 25% ICE (LIKE PLUTO)

SURFACE: COVERED WITH N_2, CH_4, CO, CO_2 ICES

ATMOSPHERE: VERY THIN, MOSTLY N_2, SOME CH_4

- THIN CLOUDS AND HAZES OBSERVED
- REDDISH COLOR: MAYBE DUE TO METHANE REACTING WITH UV
- BIG SOUTH POLAR CAP OBSERVED (N_2 PROBABLY MIGRATES FROM POLE TO POLE DURING SEASONS)
- WIND STREAKS OBSERVED IN CAPS
- GEYSER-LIKE PLUMES ALSO OBSERVED

    SOURCE OF ENERGY COULD BE TIDAL HEATING DUE TO RETROGRADE ORBIT?
- TRITON CAN BE TOGETHER WITH PLUTO LARGEST SURVIVING BODY OF ORIGINAL K.B. POPULATION

NEREID IS SMALL, DARK SATELLITE ON ECCENTRIC ORBIT, PROBABLY CAPTURED BY NEPTUNE

6 SMALL MOONS ARE CLOSE TO THE PLANET, VERY DARK HAVE REGULAR ORBITS AND SOME ASSOCIATED WITH RINGS

PLANETARY RINGS

- MADE OF SMALL PARTICLES ON INDIVIDUAL ORBITS
- ALL GIANT PLANETS HAVE RINGS

ALL RINGS ARE WITHIN ROCHE LIMIT
(EXCEPT OUTER EDGE OF SATURN'S RINGS)

ROCHE LIMIT: DISTANCE FROM A PLANET BELLOW WHICH THE DIFFERENTIAL [=TIDAL] PULL OF THE PLANET ON TWO NEIGHBORING PARTICLES EXCEEDS THEIR MUTUAL GRAVITATIONAL ATTRACTION.

$$\left(\frac{d}{R}\right)_{Roche} \simeq 2.5 \left(\frac{\rho_p}{\rho_s}\right)^{1/3}$$

d - distance of R.L.
R - Planetary radius
ρ_p & ρ_s - densities of planet and particles

MEANING: NO SATELLITES CAN FORM WITHIN R.L.

GAPS CAN BE PRODUCED BY MOONS BY MEANS OF:
1. RESONANCES (GAPS ARE CREATED IN PLACES THAT HAVE ORBITAL PERIOD THAT IS SIMPLE FRACTION OF MOON'S)
2. ORBITING WITHIN RINGS AND SWEEPING MATERIAL

NARROW RINGS CAN BE MAINTAINED BY
1. SHEPHERDING: THE RING IS HELD IN PLACE BY TWO MOONS ORBITING CLOSELY ON EACH SIDE
2. 'CRUMBLING' OF A MOON THAT SUPPLIES MATERIAL TO THE RING

Life in the Solar System:

Places Where People Thought there is life:
- Sun (Herschel 1795) impossible Too Hot!
- Moon but No Atmosphere!
- Life like us on Mars: Civilization building Channels
- Life Arising in Comets or Asteroids: disapproved today. But life may have traveled in them.

Places Where People still think there is/was life:
- Titan: Organic Material on Surface – Could evolve into life?
- Europa: Liquid Water under Ice. Could life evolve there?
- Ancient Life on Mars?
    - Meteorites can travel from Mars to Earth
    - Gas trapped inside Meteorite → Gives hints to primitive martian atmosphere
    - Meteorite Alan Hills 84001 contains structures that may be primitive life. (They may also have formed Abiologically)

GLOSSARY OF LUNAR SCIENCE

A

ALBEDO
Relative brightness. It is the ratio of the amount of electromagnetic radiation reflected by a body to the amount of incident radiation.

ALPHA PARTICLE
A positive particle consisting of 2 protons and 2 neutrons. It is the nucleus of a helium atom.

ANGSTROM UNIT
A unit of length equal to 10^{-10} meters or 10^{-4} microns. It is approximately, four-billionths of an inch. In solids, such as salt, iron, aluminum, the distance between atoms is usually a few Angstroms.

APERTURE
A small opening such as a camera shutter through which light rays pass to expose film when the shutter is open.

ATTENUATION
Decrease in intensity usually of such wave phenomena as light or sound.

B

BASALT
A type of dark gray rock formed by solidification of molten material. The rocks of Hawaii are basalts.

BISTATIC RADAR
The electrical properties of the Moon's surface can be measured by studying the characteristics of radio waves reflected from the Moon. If the radio transmitter and receiver are located at the same place, the term monostatic radar is used. If they are located at different places, then bistatic is used. In the study of the Moon with bistatic radar, the transmitter is aboard the CSM and the receiver is on the Earth.

BRECCIA
A coarse-grained rock composed of angular fragments of pre-existing rocks.

BOUNDARY LAYER
The interaction layer between the solar wind bow shock and the magnetopause.

BOW SHOCK
The shock wave produced by the interaction of the solar wind with the Earth's magnetosphere.

C

CARTOGRAPHY
The production and science of accurately scaled maps.

CASSETTE
Photographic film container. Also magnetic tape container.

CISLUNAR
Pertaining to the space between the Earth and Moon or the Moon's orbit.

COLLIMATOR
A device for producing beams of parallel rays of light or other electromagnetic radiation.

COLORIMETRIC
Pertaining to the measurement of the intensities of different colors as of lunar surface materials.

COSMIC RAYS
Streams of very high energy nuclear particles, commonly protons, that bombard the Earth and Moon from all directions.

COSMOLOGY
Study of the character and origin of the universe.

CRATER
A naturally occurring hole. On Earth, a very few craters are formed by meteorites striking the Earth; most are caused by volcanoes. On the Moon, most craters were caused by meteorites. Sohe lunar craters were apparently formed by volcanic processes. In the formation of lunar craters, large blocks of rock (perhaps as large as several hundred meters across) are thrown great distances from the crater. These large blocks in turn form craters also -- such craters are termed secondary craters.

CROSS-SUN
A direction approximately 90 degrees to the direction of the Sun and related to lunar surface photography.

CROSSTRACK.
Perpendicular to the instantaneous direction of a spacecraft's ground track.

CRYSTALLINE ROCKS
Rocks consisting wholly or chiefly of mineral crystals. Such rocks on the Moon are usually formed by cooling from a liquid melt.

D

DIELECTRIC
A material that is an electrical insulator. Most rocks are dielectrics.

DIURNAL
Recurring daily. Diurnal processes on Earth repeat themselves every 24 hours but on the Moon repeat every 28 Earth days. The length of a lunar day is 28 Earth days.

DOPPLER TRACKING
A system for measuring the trajectory of spacecraft from Earth using continuous radio waves and the Doppler effect. An example of the Doppler effect is the change in pitch of a train's whistle and a car's horn on passing an observer. Because of this effect, the frequency of the radio waves received on Earth is changed slightly by the velocity of the spacecraft in exactly the same way that the pitch of a train's whistle is changed by the velocity of the train.

DOWN-SUN
In the direction that is directly away from the Sun and related to lunar surface photography.

E

EARTHSHINE
Illumination of the Moon's surface by sunlight reflected from the Earth. The intensity is many times smaller than that of the direct sunlight.

ECLIPTIC PLANE
The plane defined by the Earth's orbit about the Sun.

EFFLUENT
Any liquid or gas discharged from a spacecraft such as waste water, urine, fuel cell purge products, etc.; also any material discharged from volcanoes.

EGRESS
A verb meaning to exit or to leave. The popularization of this word has been attributed to the great showman P.T. Barnum, who reportedly discovered that a sign marked exit had almost no effect on the large crowds that accumulated in his exhibit area but a sign marked *to egree* led the crowds outdoors. In space terminology, it means simply to leave the spacecraft.

EJECTA
Lunar material thrown out (as resulting from meteoroid impact or volcanic action).

ELECTRON
A small fundamental particle with a unit of negative electrical charge, a very small mass, and a very small diameter. Every atom contains one or more electrons. The proton is the corresponding elementary particle with a unit of positive charge and a mass of 1,837 times as great as the mass of the electron.

EXOSPHERE
The outermost portion of the Earth's or Moon's atmosphere from which gases can escape into outer space.

F

FIELD
A region in which each point has a definite value such as magnetic field.

FIELD OF VIEW
The region *seen* by the camera lens and recorded on the film. The same phrase is applied to such other equipment as radar and radio antennas.

FILLET
Debris (soil) piled against a rock; several scientists have suggested that the volume of the fillet may be directly proportional to the time the rock has been in its present position and to the rock size.

FLUORESCENCE
Emission of radiation at one wavelength in response to the absorption of energy at a different wavelength. Some lunar materials fluoresce. Most do not. The process is identical to that of the familiar fluorescent lamps.

FLUX
The rate of flow per unit area of some quantity such as the flux of cosmic rays or the flux of particles in the solar wind.

FRONT
The more or less linear outer slope of a mountain range that rises above a plain or plateau. In the United States, the Colorado Front Range is a good example.

G

GALACTIC
Pertaining to a galaxy in the universe such as the Milky Way.

GAMMA
A measure of magnetic field strength; the Earth's magnetic field is about 50,000 gamma. The Moon's magnetic field is only a few gamma.

GAMMA-RAY
One of the rays emitted by radioactive substances. Gamma rays are highly penetrating and can traverse several centimeters of lead.

GARDENING
The overturning, reworking, and changing of the lunar surface due to such processes as meteoroid impact, volcanic action, aging and such.

GEGENSCHEIN
A faint light covering a 20 degree field-of-view projected on the celestial sphere about the Sun-Earth vector (as viewed from the dark side of the Earth).

GEOCHEMICAL GROUP
A group of three experiments especially designed to study the chemical composition of the lunar surface remotely from lunar orbit.

GEODESY
Originally, the science of the exact size and shape of the Earth; recently broadened in meaning to include the Moon and other planets.

GEOPHONE
A small device implanted in the lunar surface during the deployment of the ASE to detect vibrations of the Moon from artificial and natural sources.

GEOPHYSICS
Physics of planetary bodies, such as the Earth and Moon, and the surrounding environment; the many branches include gravity, magnetism, heat flow, seismology, space physics, geodesy, meteorology, and sometimes geology.

GNOMON
A rod mounted on a tripod in such a way that it is free to swing in any direction and indicates the local vertical; it gives Sun position and serves as size scale. Color and reflectance scales are provided on the rod and a colorimetric reference is mounted on one leg.

GRADIENT
The rate of change of something with distance. Mathematically, it is the space rate of change of a function. For example, the slope of a mountain is the gradient of the elevation.

I

IMBRIAN AGE
Two methods of measuring age on the Moon are used. One provides the absolute age, in years, and is based on radioactivity. The other gives only relative ages. A very old event on the Moon is that which produced the Imbrium basin. The age of other geologic features can be determined with respect to the Imbrium event.

INGRESS
A verb meaning to enter. It is used in connection with entering the LM. See also EGRESS.

IN SITU
Literally, *in place, in its original position.* For example, taking photographs of a lunar surface rock sample *in situ* (as it lies on the surface).

LIMB
The outer edge of the apparent disk of a celestial body, as the Moon or Earth, or a portion of the edge.

LITHOLOGY
The character of a rock formation.

LUNATION
One complete passage of the Moon around its orbit.

M

MANTLE
An intermediate layer of the Moon between the outer layer and the central core.

MARE
A large dark flat area on the lunar surface (Lunar Sea). May be seen with the unaided eye.

MARIA
Plural of mare.

MASCOONS
Large mass concentrations beneath the surface of the Moon. They were discovered only 3 years ago by changes induced by them in the precise orbits of spacecraft about the Moon.

MASS SPECTROMETER
An instrument which distinguishes chemical species in terms of their different isotopic masses.

METEORITE
A solid body that has arrived on the Earth or Moon from outer space. It can range in size from microscopic to many tons. Its composition ranges from that of silicate rocks to metallic iron-nickel.

METRIC PHOTOGRAPHY
Recording of surface topography by means of photography, together with an appropriate network of coordinates, to form the basis of accurate measurements and reference points for precise photographic mapping.

MICROSCOPIC
Of such a size as to be invisible to the unaided eye but readily visible through a microscope.

MINERALOGY
The science of minerals; deals with the study of their atomic structure and their general physical and chemical properties.

MONOPOLE
All known magnets have two poles, one south pole and one north pole. The existence of a single such pole, termed a monopole, has not yet been established but is believed by many physicists to exist on the basis of theoretical studies. Lunar samples have been carefully searched on Earth for the presence of monopoles.

MORPHOLOGY
The external shape of rocks in relation to the development of erosional forms or topographic features.

MOULTON POINT
A theoretical point along the Sun-Earth line located 940,000 statute miles from the Earth at which the sum of all gravitational forces is zero.

N

NADIR
That point on the Earth (or Moon) vertically below the observer.

NAUTICAL MILE
It is 6,280 feet -- 19 percent larger than a *regular* mile.

NEUTRON
An uncharged elementary particle that has a mass nearly equal to that of a proton and is present in all known atomic nuclei except hydrogen.

O

OCCULTATION
The disappearance of a body behind another body of larger apparent size. For example, the occultation of the Sun by the Moon as viewed by an Earth observer to create a solar eclipse.

OZONE
Triatomic oxygen (O_3); found in significant quantities in the Earth's atmosphere.

P

P-10
A gas mixture consisting of 90 percent argon, 9.5 percent carbon dioxide, and 0.5 percent helium used to fill the x-ray detectors of the x-ray fluorescence experiment.

PANORAMA
A series of photographs taken from a point to cover 360 degrees around that point.

PENUMBRA
The part of a shadow in which the light (or other rays such as the solar wind) is only partially masked, in contrast to the umbra in which light is completely masked by the intervening object.

PETROGRAPHY
Systematic description of rocks based on observations in the field (e.g., on the Moon), on returned specimens, and on microscopic work.

PHOTOMULTIPLIER TUBE
An electron tube that produces electrical signals in response to light. In the tube, the signal is amplified to produce a measurable output current from very small quantities of light.

PLASMA
A gas composed of ions, electrons, neutral atoms, and molecules. The interactions between particles is mainly electromagnetic. Although the individual particles are electrically positive or negative, the gas as a whole is neutral.

POSIGRADE
Lunar orbital motion in the direction of lunar rotation.

PRIMORDIAL
Pertaining to the earliest, or original, lunar rocks that were created during the time between the initial and final formation stages of the Moon.

PROTON
The positively charged constituent of atomic nuclei.

R

RADON
Isotopes of a radioactive gaseous element with atomic number 86 and atomic masses of 220 and 222 formed by the radioactive decay of radium.

RAY
Bright material that extends radially from many craters on the Moon, believed to have been formed at the same time as the associated
craters were formed by impacting objects from space; usually, but not always, arcs of great circles. They may be several hundred kilometers long.

REGOLITH
The unconsolidated residual material that resides on the solid surface of the Moon (or Earth).

RETROGRADE
Lunar orbital motion opposite the direction of lunar rotation.

RILLE/RILL
A long, narrow valley on the Moon's surface.

RIM
Elevated region around craters and rilles.

S

SAMPLE
Small quantities of lunar soil or rocks that are sufficiently small to return them to Earth. On each mission several different kinds of samples are collected. Contingency sample consists of 1 to 2 pounds of rocks and soil collected very early in the surface operations so that at least some material will have been returned to Earth in the event that the surface activities are halted abruptly and the mission aborted. Documented sample is one that is collected with a full set of photographs to allow positive identification of the sample when returned to Earth with the sample in situ together with a complete verbal description by the astronaut. Comprehensive sample is a documented sample collected over an area of a few yards square.

S-BAND
A range of frequencies used in radar and communications that extends from 1.55 to 5.2 kilomegahertz.

SCARP
A line of cliffs produced by faulting or erosion.

SEISMIC
Related to mechanical vibration within the Earth or Moon resulting from, for example, impact of meteoroids on the surface.

SHOCKED ROCKS
Rocks which have been formed by or subjected to the extremes of temperature and pressure from impacts.

SOLAR WIND
Streams of particles (mostly hydrogen and helium) emanating from and flowing approximately radially outward from the Sun.

SPATIAL
Pertaining to the location of points in three-dimensional space; contrasted with temporal (pertaining to time) locations.

SPECTROMETER
An instrument which separates radiation into energy bands (or, in a mass spectrometer, particles into mass groups) and indicates the relative intensities in each band or group.

SPUR
A ridge of lesser elevation that extends laterally from a mountain or mountain range.

STELLAR
Of or pertaining to stars.

STEREO
A type of photography in which photographs taken of the same area from different angles are combined to produce visible features in three-dimensional relief.

SUPPLEMENTARY SAMPLE STOP
A stop added to a traverse after the stations are numbered. Mission planning continues through launch and the supplementary sample stops are inserted between normal traverse stations.

SUPRATHERMAL
Having energies greater than thermal energy.

SUBSATELLITE
A small unmanned satellite, deployed from the spacecraft while it is in orbit, designed to obtain various types of solar wind, lunar magnetic, and S-band tracking data over an extended period of time.

T

TALUS
Rock debris accumulated at the base of a cliff by erosion of material from higher elevation.

TEMPORAL
Referring to the passage or measurement of time.

TERMINATOR
The line separating the illuminated and the darkened areas of a body such as the Earth or Moon which is not self-luminous.

TERRA
Those portions of the lunar surface other than the maria; the lighter areas of the Moon. They are visible to the unaided eye.

TIDAL
Referring to the very small movement of the surface of the Moon or the Earth due to the gravitational attraction of other planetary bodies. Similar to the oceanic tides, the solid parts of the Earth's crust rise and fall twice daily about three feet. Lunar tides are somewhat larger. The tides of solid bodies are not felt by people but are easily observed with instruments.

TIMELINE
A detailed schedule of astronaut or mission activities indicating the activity and time at which it occurs within the mission.

TOPOGRAPHIC
Pertaining to the accurate graphical description, usually on maps or charts, of the physical features of an area on the Earth or Moon.

TRANSEARTH
During transit from the Moon to the Earth.

TRANSIENT
A short-lived event that does not repeat at regular intervals, often occurring in a system when first turned on and before reaching operating equilibrium. For example, the initial current surge that occurs when an electrical system is energized.

TRANSPONDER
A combined receiver and transmitter whose function is to transmit signals automatically when triggered by a suitable signal. Those used in space are sensitive to radio signals.

U

UMBRA
The dark central portion of the shadow of a large body such as the Earth or Moon. Compare penumbra.

UP-SUN
Into the direction of the Sun and related to lunar surface photography.

URANIUM
One of the heavy metallic elements that are radioactive.

V

VECTOR
A quantity that requires both magnitude and direction for its specification, as velocity, magnetic force field, and gravitational acceleration vectors.

WAVELENGTH
The distance between peaks (or minima) of waves such as ocean waves or electromagnetic waves.

X

X-RAY
Electromagnetic radiation of non-nuclear origin within the wavelength interval of 0.1 to 100 Angstroms (between gamma ray and ultraviolet radiation), x-rays are used in medicine to examine teeth, lungs, bones, and other parts of the human body; they also occur naturally.

Z

ZODIACAL LIGHT

A faint glow extending around the entire zodiac but showing most prominently in the neighborhood of the Sun. (It may be seen in the west after twilight and in the east before dawn as a diffuse glow. The glow may be sunlight reflected from a great number of particles of meteoritic size in or near the ecliptic in the planetoid belt.)

www.ingramcontent.com/pod-product-compliance
Lightning Source LLC
Chambersburg PA
CBHW082040300426
44117CB00015B/2548